A WEIRD AND WILD BEAUTY

A WEIRD AND WILD BEAUTY

THE STORY OF YELLOWSTONE, THE WORLD'S FIRST NATIONAL PARK

ERIN PEABODY

Sky Pony Press
New York

Sky Pony Press books may be purchased in bulk at special discounts for sales promotion, corporate gifts, fund-raising, or educational purposes. Special editions can also be created to specifications. For details, contact the Special Sales Department, Sky Pony Press, 307 West 36th Street, 11th Floor, New York, NY 10018 or info@skyhorsepublishing.com.

Sky Pony® is a registered trademark of Skyhorse Publishing, Inc.®, a Delaware corporation.

Visit our website at www.skyponypress.com.

10 9 8 7 6 5 4 3 2

Manufactured in China, October 2015
This product conforms to CPSIA 2008

Library of Congress Cataloging-in-Publication Data

Peabody, Erin.
    A weird and wild beauty : the story of Yellowstone, the world's first national park / Erin Peabody.
        pages cm

Summary: "The summer of 1871, a team of thirty-two men set out on the first scientific expedition across Yellowstone. Through uncharted territory, some of the day's most renowned scientists and artists explored, sampled, sketched, and photographed the region's breathtaking wonders—from its white-capped mountain vistas and thundering falls to its burping mud pots and cauldrons of molten magma. At the end of their adventure, the survey packed up their specimens and boarded trains headed east, determined to convince Congress that the country needed to preserve the land from commercial development. They returned with 'stories of wonder hardly short of fairy tales,' to quote the New York Times. With the support of conservationists such as Ralph Waldo Emerson, Henry David Thoreau, Frederick Law Olmsted, and John Muir, the importance of a national park was secured. On March 1, 1872, Ulysses S. Grant signed the Yellowstone Park Bill into law. It set aside over two million acres of one-of-a-kind wilderness as 'a great national park for the benefit and enjoyment of people.' This important and fascinating book will introduce young adults to the astonishing adventure that led to 'the best idea America ever had.' Today over 130 countries have copied the Yellowstone model, and billions of acres of critical habitat and spectacular scenery are being preserved for all of us to enjoy. This book has a wonderful ecological and historical message for readers ages 12 and up. No book about Yellowstone's founding has been written for this age group before, yet Yellowstone National Park is a major destination for many families, so many readers will likely have heard of Yellowstone or even have visited there. This is a great book for any school library or for history or science classrooms in middle and high school, where information can be used for research projects"—Provided by publisher.

    Audience: Grades 7 to 8.
    Includes bibliographical references and index.
    ISBN 978-1-63450-204-7
    (print)—ISBN 978-1-63450-935-0 (ebook)
    1. Yellowstone National Park—History—Juvenile literature. 2. Yellowstone National Park—Discovery and exploration—Juvenile literature. 3. Yellowstone National Park—Environmental conditions—Juvenile literature. 4. National parks and reserves—
United States—History—Juvenile literature. 5. Landscape protection—United States—History—Juvenile literature. I. Title.
    F722.P34 2016
    978.7'52—dc23
                                2015035831

Cover design by Sarah Brody
Cover photo credit Thinkstock

CONTENTS

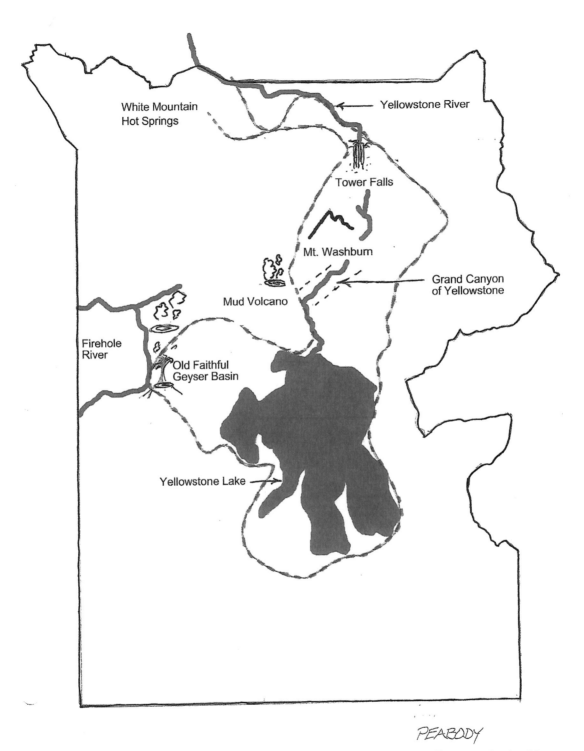

White Mountain Hot Springs

Yellowstone River

Tower Falls

Mt. Washburn

Mud Volcano

Grand Canyon of Yellowstone

Firehole River

Old Faithful Geyser Basin

Yellowstone Lake

PEABODY

The red dotted line represents the Hayden Expedition's route through Yellowstone in 1871. Map by Ryan Peabody.

PROLOGUE
DISBELIEF

While you see and wonder, you seem to need an additional sense . . . to comprehend and believe.

—Nathaniel Langford, explorer in Yellowstone

NEW YORK CITY, WINTER 1870 – 71

J. G. Holland sat at his desk, staring wide-eyed at the pages spread before him. Holland was an editor at *Scribner's Monthly*, a popular magazine and source of news for Americans in the mid- to late 1800s.[1]

Holland had just received the most bizarre-sounding account. It spoke of a strange land where the ground gurgled and hissed. A land where scalding waters blew from craters and vats of steaming pink mud threatened to swallow a man whole. The place, according to the man who'd recently traveled through the region, abounded with "boiling springs," "mud volcanoes," and "huge mountains of sulphur."[2]

Incredulous, Holland tried to absorb the dazzling imagery. The author, clearly spellbound by what he saw, gushed about brilliant turquoise pools and hot-water fountains. The mud volcano, the man wrote, erupted with the force of thundering cannons. Its boiling broth scalded trees hundreds of yards away.[3]

This world of absurdities, the traveler informed Holland, was not some far-off land. It belonged to the United States.

J. G. Holland, editor at *Scribner's Monthly* magazine, opened himself to criticism when he published a jaw-dropping account on the wonders of Yellowstone in 1871. The journalist died ten years later with the phrase "to devote life to truth" etched in Latin on his gravestone.

Artist's woodcut of a "mud volcano" appearing in *Scribner's Monthly.*

The mysterious high-mountain region lay just south of the sprawling Montana Territory. By the 1860s, as increasing numbers of settlers infiltrated the western half of the country, this area remained one of the last unexplored pockets left in the West.[4] Its location, if it even appeared on maps, was marked by only two haunting words: *terra incognita*, which is Latin for "unknown land."[5]

Impenetrable snow and ice, as well as fears about hostile Native tribes, had kept men from exploring this region, as had rumors about the area's infernal boilers that supposedly belched steam, reeked of death, and harbored sinister spirits.

Scribner's—similar to today's *Time* or *Life* magazines—was a common fixture in American households in the nineteenth century. Readers prized its lavish illustrations (as photographs were still a rare treat) and rushed to read its latest features on history, science, religion, and art. And by the 1860s, travel writing had become popular, especially stories about America's exotic western frontier.

To most Easterners living and working in cramped, smoke-filled factory towns, the American West—with its dramatic scenery, invigorating air, and populations

The first issue of the monthly periodical *Scribner's Monthly.*

Images, like this painting by Albert Bierstadt, drew Americans westward.

of curious indigenous people—seemed unusual, enticing, and bursting with possibility.

Ever since the trailblazers Meriwether Lewis and William Clark shared the fascinating details of their daring journey in 1804 across the country to the Pacific Ocean and back, Americans had craved details about the little-known western half of their country.

Scribner's readers tracked the progress of western adventurers such as John C. Fremont with great excitement. His gritty accounts of scaling mountains and surviving blazing desert heat appeared in the nation's newspapers as well as the penny press, a tabloid-style paper that sold for a penny a piece and made news affordable for the working class.

Western explorer John C. Fremont.

City dwellers envied the freedom of explorers like Fremont. "What a wild life," wrote poet Henry Wadsworth Longfellow about Fremont's heroic rambles across the West, "and what a fresh kind of existence!"[6]

By the 1870s, the nation was also eager to escape the dark gloom cast by the recent Civil War. Thousands of families had lost loved ones: more than six hundred thousand American soldiers had perished in the four-year war. Cities and local economies had been ravaged by the fighting. Amid all of this, the wide blue skies of the West emanated hope for the nation's downtrodden.

Holland continued to consider the colorful account he had received. What could be more exciting to readers than details about a yet-discovered American territory where hot waters leaped from the ground and steaming, blue pools funneled deep into the Earth? Yet, how absurd it all sounded. Bubbling pink mud? Jetting fountains? Could such a place truly exist?

As a journalist, Holland also had to consider the reputation of the magazine. Should he take a chance on such sensational-sounding material?

The account's author, Nathaniel Langford, was evidently well educated. The former banker had moved to the Montana Territory shortly after gold was struck in the region in 1863. Furthermore, Langford was joined on his journey by several

Nathaniel Langford during the 1870 Yellowstone expedition.

other leading citizens of the Montana Territory, including a former major general in the Civil War, a journalist, and an attorney.

After much consideration, Holland decided to publish Langford's account of the peculiar paradise near the Montana Territory. The editor ultimately believed in giving his readers the intriguing stories they desired.

By the following spring, Langford's story, told in his own words, appeared in *Scribner's*. An artist was tasked with illustrating the unusual marvels the traveler had described, but with no photographs or firsthand experience to reference, the artist relied heavily on his own imagination.

Despite Langford's intelligent prose, the story about the wondrous region out West was rejected by many readers. Some wrote letters to the magazine's office, mocking the paper for printing nonsense and accusing Holland of abandoning his ethics. One reader dismissed Langford as "the champion liar of the Northwest."[7]

Many Easterners accepted that the American West was home to surprising scenery. But, for some, the land adorned with boiling craters and rocketing fountains sounded too fantastic to be true.

An artist's depiction of one of the astonishing sights—a geyser cone—described by Langford in *Scribner's Monthly.*

CHAPTER 1
HOMELAND

By the time I was forty, I could see our country was changing fast, and that these changes were causing us to live very different.[8]

—Plenty Coups, Crow chief

The absurd land that Langford described in the *Scribner's* article already had a name: Yellowstone. And it had been a home and destination for many people for thousands of years.

Mi tse a-da-zi, the earliest people called it. Meaning "Rock Yellow River," this name was used by Minnetaree American Indians to describe the large river in the area that coursed and coiled through bluffs of golden rock. French fur trappers, fanning out into the region to hunt beaver in the 1700s, translated the Native word they heard to "Roche Jaune." In English, the region, as well as the river that ran through it, became known as "Yellow Stone."[9]

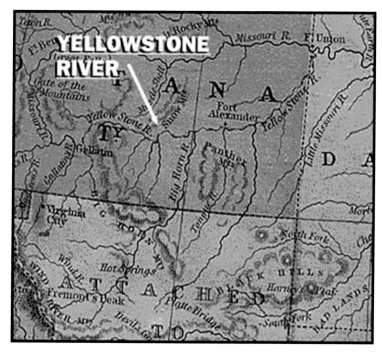

Yellowstone River running through the Wyoming and Montana Territories.

Crow Indian on the Lookout, by
Alfred Jacob Miller.

Bison, or American buffalo.

American Indians and their ancestors used Yellowstone as a hunting ground and home for at least ten thousand years.[10] Archeologists know this based on primitive tools they've discovered in the area. Yellowstone offered indigenous peoples a bounty of resources: massive herds of buffalo, elk, and sheep to hunt for food and clothing; rivers and lakes teeming with trout; and hot water springs that could be tapped for cooking, medicinal purposes, and much-needed winter warmth.

A group of Plains American Indians known as the Crow lived east of Yellowstone in parts of present-day Montana and Wyoming (where many of their descendants still reside today). Flathead and Blackfeet peoples traveled down to Yellowstone from the North, using the Yellowstone River as a guide.

These tribes created their own trails and journeyed through Yellowstone seasonally. In spring, they'd wait until the chilly tributaries of the Yellowstone River turned pink with masses of spawning cutthroat trout. In summer, they

Girls of Bannock American Indian
tribe wearing dresses ornamented
with elk teeth.

Cutthroat trout.

tracked large herds of buffalo, elk, and antelope that grazed in Yellowstone's lush green valleys. They also mined the region's rich stores of obsidian—a black glassy rock so coveted for its utility and beauty that it was traded as far east as the Ohio River Valley.

But one group of American Indians lived in Yellowstone year-round, despite the brutal winters that pummeled the region with snowpack, ice, and temperatures as cold as minus 40 degrees Fahrenheit. They were a tribe of Shoshone known as the Tukudika, or Sheepeaters.

Obsidian points.

Sought-after Stone

It's a beautiful stone—shiny and smooth like glass and as black as coal—rendered from one of the most violent processes on Earth. And Yellowstone is one of the few places in North America where this rock, called *obsidian*, is found in such great abundance.

Hundreds of thousands of years ago, massive volcanoes erupted in the Yellowstone region. Once the flaming lava from these eruptions hit the surrounding air or struck nearby lakes, rivers, or icy glaciers, it quickly cooled (think of how piping-hot molasses drizzled onto snow instantly hardens). This flash-cooling effect created entire cliffs of obsidian, a kind of volcanic glass.

Native peoples in the Yellowstone region used obsidian for arrowheads and knives. They also used it as a scraping tool for cleaning hides, for sewing, and even as a surgical tool that could cut cleanly and deeply through skin.

The reach of the American Indians' obsidian trade astounds archeologists, who've discovered pieces of the rock as far east as present-day Ohio.

These semi-nomadic people lived in family groups and moved frequently across Yellowstone and the surrounding land. Their shelters, teepee-shaped "wickiups" made of propped-up limbs and sticks, could be easily relocated as families journeyed across the region. Sheepeaters never adopted the horse but instead relied on their dogs—beasts of burden as well as cherished pets—to transport foods and household goods.

Sheepeater family.

Wickiup, or Sheepeater shelter.

Sheepeaters' Canines

Smaller than today's huskies, the Sheepeaters' dogs were a vital part of their culture and lifestyle. Even after the horse arrived on the Great Plains and was adopted by other Native tribes, the Sheepeaters continued to rely on their dogs for transportation and companionship.

Sturdy and compact, dogs could be outfitted with leather packs or tethered to a small sled or travois to haul children and supplies. The dogs were a perfect size for shuttling household goods and food from one seasonal camp to the next. Dogs were companions as well—joining in on a hunt, alerting their owners to lurking enemy tribes, and providing a source of comfort to children.

In recent years, Yellowstone park archeologists discovered the remains of a Sheepeater man, and buried beside him was a dog—likely his cherished pet.

Sego lily.

Like our modern ecologists, the Sheepeaters knew Yellowstone across every season. They knew when the grizzly exited its wintry lair in May; when, in fall, underground bulbs of white sego lilies swelled into potato-like nuggets and were ready to be dug up and eaten; and when the roaring waterfalls of summer quieted in the deep freeze of winter.

The tribe subsisted largely on the meat of bighorn sheep—the large, curly-horned animals after which the Sheepeaters were named. But so many of Yellowstone's resources were edible for the Tukudika, including elk, deer, small mammals, and fish, as well as nuts, seeds, and berries. They also dug up plant roots, which they ground into flour and baked into cakes. In lean times, they stripped and ate the soft inner bark of pine trees.

Master Hunters

The Tukudika knew that in the summer months, when grizzlies and wolves stalked Yellowstone's lower valleys, bighorn sheep sought refuge by dashing to the upper reaches of nearby mountains and cliffs. With their muscular legs and flexible hooves, the sheep could traverse perilous ledges out of reach of less adept predators.

The Sheepeaters used this knowledge to invent a clever hunting strategy. If they spied a herd of sheep in a nearby valley, the Natives would send their best hunters to climb the adjacent cliffs. There the men would wait with their handmade bows, preparing to launch their arrows. Meanwhile, down below, the tribe's younger men and boys would start yipping and howling, imitating one of the sheep's top predators: wolves. Panicked, the grazing sheep would scramble up the nearby slopes, right into the hands of the poised and ready hunters.[11]

Bighorn sheep on cliffs.

Osbourne Russell, a fur trapper who crossed Yellowstone in 1835, made contact with a band of Sheepeaters. "They were all neatly clothed in dressed deer and sheepskins of the best quality," he noted in his journal, "and seemed to be perfectly contented and happy."[12] Their few material possessions included an old butcher knife, a small stone pot, as well as the thirty or so dogs that carried their food, goods, and the skins with which they traded.[13]

Russell was most impressed by the Sheep-eaters' elegant bows, made from sheep horns and adorned with porcupine quills. Ever resourceful, the Natives likely used Yellowstone's boiling springs to cook the hard horns until they were soft enough to straighten. They tipped their arrows with pointy shards of obsidian.

The Sheepeaters were master survivalists who subsisted off a land no others could. But even *they* could not adapt quickly enough to the changes that lay ahead.

Shoshone Warrior Smoking His Pipe, by Alfred Jacob Miller.

***

As more and more white settlers poured into the prairies, plains, and valleys of the American West, the treasure hunters among them became increasingly enthralled with the land's oversized resources. It wasn't long before rumors drifted back east about mountains entombed with silver and copper, giant sequoia trees that pierced the heavens, and rivers that glittered with gold.

It was the gold that made men most crazy. Nuggets of the bright shining stuff danced in the imagination of the poor and rich alike. Reports of five-pound hunks

Gold miners as depicted in an 1856 newspaper, *Ballou's Pictorial Drawing-Room Companion.*

of gold drifted from one frontier town to another, wooing people into bravery, brashness, and sheer stupidity.

In the blink of an eye, men abandoned their families and homes for a chance to make a fortune out West. It was an insatiable hunger—"gold fever" as some called it—that consumed people like a disease. According to one gold hunter, the lust for gold "buzzed about the brain and tickled in the stomach."[14] The gold miners came armed with picks, axes, and butcher knives—any tool that would pry open the earth.

Chinese gold miners at camp.

All types of people were drawn into the clanging chaos of gold rush towns. Fleeing hardship and despair, men, women, and children—from as far away as China and Australia—boarded disease- and rat-infested boats bound for America's western shores. In the United States, Civil War veterans, former slaves, and poor laborers joined them in the search for new lives, a livable income, and the promise of a better future.

Gold rush towns sprouted up like weeds across the western frontier and were shoddily built and exceedingly dirty. Flimsy wooden shacks served as general stores, banks, saloons, dance halls, and brothels. With no sewage systems, waste and excrement bubbled up on side streets. Locals strolled streets caked in manure. Boys as young as five played poker. Scrappy youngsters crawled outside the doors of banks and saloons, combing floorboards and carpets for flecks of gold.

Other resources, besides gold, were also sought by the incoming tide of settlers. Mountaintops were sheared off in the hopes of finding silver and copper. Forests were felled to make way for cities, farms, and railroads that would soon span the country. For every mile of railroad track, twenty-five hundred ties were needed—all made from wood.[15]

Logged trees.

Powerful hoses were used to excavate gold and other ores.

Mark Twain, a well-known political commentator at the time, wrote satirical columns in the nation's newspapers about America's obsession with quick money:

"What is the chief end of man?
—to get rich.

In what way?
—dishonestly if we can; honestly if we must."[16]

Americans lived by the "get what you can" principle, wrote another writer living in the gold rush town of Virginia City, Montana.[17]

Man posing with shot bison.

All of these disturbances to the natural landscape—disruptions driven by greed in many cases—sent ripples through Native peoples' homelands. The American Indians' sacred lands— places where they hunted, gathered together, and buried family members— were being transformed or utterly destroyed.

At the time, treaties were being drawn up by the US government to appease tribes, though most of them proved worthless. These official government documents were often rescinded or rewritten to benefit the large and powerful businesses of the era, such as oil, steel, and railroad companies, and Native peoples found themselves kicked out of their homelands.

As their anger grew, tribes retaliated, sometimes violently. White and European settlers feared American Indian attacks as they crossed the West on wagon and horseback. Many viewed the Natives as "savages," "beasts," and "degrades," terms used by white Americans well into the 1900s.

Settlers spoke of ridding their towns of the American Indian "pestilence." An editorial in the 1867 *Idaho Statesman* offered a solution to the "Indian problem":

> Let all the hostile bands [of Indians] be called in to attend a grand treaty; plenty of blankets and nice little trinkets distributed among them; plenty of grub on hand; have a jolly time with them; then just before the big feast put strychnine in their meat and poison to death the last mother's son of them.[18]

Nez Perce camp near Yellowstone River.

One congressman in Montana declared his hatred of Natives in the 1868 *Congressional Globe*:

I have never in my life seen a good Indian (and I have seen thousands) except when I have seen a dead Indian. I believe in the policy that exterminates the Indians, drives them outside the boundaries of civilization . . .[19]

Sadly, by 1871, opinions had not changed. Anti–American Indian attitudes persisted, and tribal lands continued to be trespassed upon. The US government provided few, if any, protections for the territorial lands being taken or for the Native peoples being killed.

Tribes in and around the Montana Territory watched as more white men probed the enchanted Yellowstone Valley. One group in particular was prepared to defend its beloved homeland.

CHAPTER 2
WAITING FOR PROOF

"Colter's Hell" sounded so much like one of Marco Polo's yarns in a thirteenth-century Venetian drawing room. [20]

—William H. Jackson, American photographer
on the skepticism surrounding Yellowstone

WASHINGTON, DC, JANUARY 19, 1871

The crowd eagerly awaited the evening's next speaker. Sitting in plush seats beneath a twinkling glass chandelier, a group of curious Americans assembled in Washington, DC's radiant Lincoln Hall to hear about a land of freakish marvels.

They had come to learn about Yellowstone. According to the *Washington Star*, that evening's lecture pertained to a mysterious region in the West that fumed with "active volcanoes, fountains of boiling water." [21] Tickets for the event cost fifty cents. [22]

How far-fetched the place sounded to many Americans. But also, how thrilling it would be for the country if even *half* of the details proved true.

Interior of Lincoln Hall, 1880.

A powerful man, Speaker of the House James G. Blaine, took center stage. He had agreed, as a special favor, to welcome the much-anticipated guest. Blaine fulfilled his promise heartily. As the crowd clapped and gaslights softly flickered, a tall man with dark eyes and a neatly trimmed beard stepped forward.

"I appear before you this evening," the stranger began, "to tell you of wonders that I have seen." [23]

Nathaniel Langford.

The speaker, whom the packed auditorium had come to see, was none other than Nathaniel Langford, back from his recent trip to the mysterious Yellowstone region.

Langford admitted to the crowd that months ago, he would have been too embarrassed to speak of a place as absurd-sounding as Yellowstone, for fear of losing his reputation. But now, he declared, there was no denying the place existed: he'd seen its astonishing sights with his own eyes.

Langford went on to tell the rapt audience—which included politicians, dignitaries, university professors, and curious citizens—about his team's harrowing journey and how it all began.

Shortly after moving to Montana Territory, Langford started hearing "strange and marvelous" stories about the region to the south.[24] Old timers in town, grizzled mountain men who'd roamed the western Rockies decades before mining towns had been established there, referred to places with names such as Hot Spring Brimstone, Burnt Hole, and Devil's Slide.

Many of these men were fur trappers, caught up in the intense, multinational hunt for beaver that swept across the western United States in the 1830s and '40s. Most of them worked for British, French, and American fur companies that competed with one another to net the most furs and pelts.

The reason the beaver was so coveted—and almost hunted to extinction in the country—was its unique fur. Not only was the fur soft and downy, capable of being woven into a fine silklike material, but it was also durably waterproof. The fur that kept beavers

Fur trapper.

The Price of Fashion

When it came to mid-1800s headwear, satiny top hats were all the rage. But the trend had rippling impacts. The fur for the hats, prized for its softness and water-repellency, came from beavers. As a result, these animals, in both Europe and North America, were nearly hunted to extinction.

There was also a human toll associated with the fashion icon. Transforming the thick fur into silky hat material was grueling work, often performed by women laboring in dangerous factory conditions for measly wages. For hours a day, laborers plucked away at pelts, removing all the coarser guard hairs until the fur was soft and smooth.

Later on, when chemicals, such as mercury, were used to expedite the process, workers traded tediousness for toxicity as they breathed in noxious fumes that caused headaches, respiratory problems, tremors, and even paralysis of the limbs. Mercury poisoning was also blamed for psychological illnesses including dementia and insanity, giving rise to the expression "mad as a hatter."

insulated and dry in their damp underwater homes was soon recognized worldwide as the finest hat material.

Beaver was the basis for many of the most popular hat styles of the eighteenth and nineteenth centuries—from Napoleon's famous tricorn to Abraham Lincoln's trademark stovepipe. By the 1860s and '70s, the lustrous black top hat—woven from beaver and silk—was the classic head topper for millionaires such as Andrew Carnegie, Cornelius Vanderbilt, and John D. Rockefeller.

Trappers were hardy adventurous types who craved freedom and the chance to explore the sprawling mountains, valleys, and rivers of the still-wild frontier. They were usually draped head to toe in a variety of skins—buffalo, antelope, otter, deer, elk, and sheep—and carried multiple rifles and traps.

A trapper's day was long and filled with dangers. For twenty miles, a trapper might journey through

John D. Rockefeller with his son, John D. Rockefeller, Jr., each sporting the iconic tophat.

Trappers around a campfire.

rain, sleet, snow, or ice, setting traps and checking on ones already laid. Even in winter the sun was brutal, as its glaring rays bounced off the snow and caused temporary blindness.

A trapper's most vital possession, his horse, was especially vulnerable on these treks. Horses fell from treacherous cliffs, were stolen by angered Natives, or fled in the night—spooked by prowling mountain lions, grizzlies, and wolves.

When a trapper finally did find a place to rest for the evening, he'd sit beside a crackling fire, gulp down the meat of an elk or deer, and finish off the day with some watered-down coffee.

If a trapper was lucky, his companions would join him. Then, they would chuckle and guffaw late into the night, swigging from bottles of whiskey and swapping stories that, according to one trapper, even the novelist Jonathan Swift could not have imagined.[25]

Some of those stories centered on an eerie place that one young trapper believed was inhabited by the devil.

The trapper was nineteen-year-old Joe Meek. Rebelling against his family and church, the young Virginian man had escaped west to wander the woods in freedom. He became a trapper and was soon introduced to the occupation's charms—and terrors.

On one trip near the Montana Territory, Meek's party was attacked by a band of armed Blackfeet American Indians. Terrified, the novice trapper fled for cover. Unfortunately, Meek's escape route sent him racing through a dark and alien landscape that left him only more traumatized.

"Behold!" Meek later wrote to a friend. "The whole country . . . was smoking with the vapor from boiling springs, and burning with gases." It was Hell, thought poor Meek, who swore he'd witnessed "blue flames and molten brimstone."[26] In truth, the dogged drifter had wandered into Yellowstone.

Several days later, two seasoned trappers found Meek and returned him to camp. The young man was unscathed, but rattled. Many

Trapper Joseph Meek.

would have dismissed Meek's story out of hand, had it not been for a host of similar trapper tales.

Old Man of the Mountains, Jim Bridger.

Another account came from Daniel Potts, a trapper who traveled through Yellowstone in 1827. In a letter to his brother, he wrote about a "mush-pot" filled with beautiful white and pink clay, and craters that erupted "pure suphor [sulfur]."[27]

Then there was trapper Warren Angus Ferris, who complained of insomnia every time he journeyed through Yellowstone. He claimed it was the noisy hot springs that kept him up, which roared through the night.[28]

But no one's stories gripped Langford more than those of weathered mountain man Jim Bridger, who Langford met in 1866. Originally from Virginia, the sixty-seven-year-old had been trapping since he was seventeen. Over the years, Bridger had served as an army scout and

American Indian interpreter, and had also built his own trading post. Located in today's Wyoming, Fort Bridger supplied weary travelers with vital goods as they journeyed westward on the Oregon Trail.

Bridger was over six feet tall, with light-gray eyes, protruding jaw bones, and a sprout of gray chin whiskers that receded into a deeply wrinkled neck. Known to friends as Old Gabe, Bridger was best known for his colorful tales—stories that were ridiculed as nonsense by some listeners.

But Bridger didn't care. He would just jabber on about the place "where hell bubbled up."[29] He also raved about forests in Yellowstone that had turned to stone. "Come with me to the Yellowstone next summer," he reportedly told a friend, "and I'll show you peetrified trees a-growing, with peetrified birds on 'em a-singing peetrified songs."[30]

There was also a virtual kitchen there, said Bridger, where a man could yank up a trout from the river and cook it in a nearby boiling spring—without ever taking it off the hook. According to Bridger, Yellowstone also possessed a canyon that was so deep a man who hollered into it at night could wake up to his own echo the next morning.

Many discounted such tales, considering trappers like Bridger little more than illiterate fools. But that didn't stop the whispers and wondering about the mythical Yellowstone.

As Langford explained to the hushed crowd before him, Yellowstone's magic had leaked out. It was enough to prompt him to plot the first organized exploration into the area.

★★★

But Langford's plans for a Yellowstone expedition were stymied from the start: he couldn't find enough men to join him. Most of the white population in the Montana Territory desperately feared American Indians. They'd heard frightful reports of early-morning ambushes and gruesome scalpings occurring at camp or along the trail.

Even the hardiest frontiersmen had grave doubts about the expedition. James Stuart, a tough and seasoned gold hunter, believed Langford's proposed journey amounted to a suicide mission. "I am just damned fool enough to go anywhere," he told expedition planners in a letter, "only I want it understood that very likely some of us will lose our hair."[31]

Officer and Author

Lieutenant Gustavus Doane, a former Union soldier in the Civil War who later became a frontier officer, provided protection to the Langford-Washburn party as they journeyed through Yellowstone in 1870.

With Doane's assistance, the party got much more than it bargained for. The battle-proven soldier, who grew up reading the swashbuckling adventures of western explorers like John Fremont, was so enchanted by Yellowstone's mind-boggling marvels that in addition to his military duties he also served as the expedition's impromptu journalist.

Lieutenant Gustavus Doane.

Doane wrote daily about the strange and mesmerizing sights the group encountered, including hot springs that sizzled with a "frying sound" and a sultry landscape that oozed "sickening and purgatorial smells."[32]

An amateur naturalist, Doane also documented the scores of wild plants and animals the party encountered. He noted ferns, huckleberries, and thimbleberries, and listed the water birds he spied on Yellowstone Lake, including swans, pelicans, gulls, and Canadian geese. He also wrote about mountain lions whose cries echoed "through the heavy forest with a peculiar, wild, and mournful sound."[33]

Mountain lion.

Doane's Yellowstone account was eventually published by the US War Department and distributed to Congress. Excerpts also appeared in a few US newspapers, providing Americans with one of the first glimpses of the bewildering geyser region.

Ultimately, a party of nineteen Montana citizens, including soldiers from the US army, volunteered to go on Langford's 1870 expedition. The group included an attorney, a newspaper correspondent, and a tax collector—men hardly suited for an intensive wilderness experience. Fortunately, Henry D. Washburn, a former major general in the Civil War, agreed to lead the group of mostly untested voyagers, providing much-needed leadership and survival skills.

Henry D. Washburn.

Two African Americans also joined the group, but were known only by their first names: Nute and Johnny. Because of their skin color, the men could only serve as camp cooks—an important role, nonetheless. They brought their dog, Booby, along, too.[34]

***

Langford had now arrived at the most thrilling part of his lecture. Listeners in the crowd held their breath as the traveler recounted the dazzling wonders the men saw.

There was the Yellowstone River, he said, whose waters raced between "enormous granite jaws."[35] There was a large jutting rock near a waterfall that they called Devil's Hoof. There were sizzling springs of a "villainous odor," including one filled with slime that reminded Langford of "mucilage."[36]

And then, just as quickly as the scenery had turned eerie and dark, it brightened. A giant pastel canyon loomed before the men. And later, large shooting fountains made Langford think of angels. "We had within a distance of fifty miles," he told the audience, "seen the greatest wonders on the continent."[37]

Yellowstone's canyon.

Of course, Langford's party had also experienced their share of distress. There were mosquito swarms, food shortages, and burns incurred from the boiling waters. Even Booby the dog was outfitted with moccasins to shield its feet from the scorching earth.

But no man left Yellowstone more traumatized than Montana tax collector, Truman Everts.

His agonizing trial began one evening when the group was setting up camp. All hands were busy—unpacking mules and horses, pitching tents, starting fires—when one of the men realized that Everts was missing.

It was typical on western expeditions for members of a party to split up. A couple of men might explore a creek while another climbed a mountaintop. So Langford and the others weren't initially alarmed by Everts's absence. He would return sooner or later, they figured.

But after a week passed without any sign of the tax collector, the party ramped up its search efforts. They fired shots in the air, scattered little bundles of dried foods and matches throughout the surrounding woods, and built fires along the high ridges near camp, hoping the smoke signals would catch Everts's attention.

Meanwhile, the wandering Everts was struggling to survive, a victim of his harsh surroundings and terrible luck. On only the second day of the ordeal, Everts lost his horse. He had dismounted briefly to explore a nearby vantage point when the animal suddenly bolted. The horse charged off, taking with it Everts's most critical supplies: his gun, blankets, and matches.

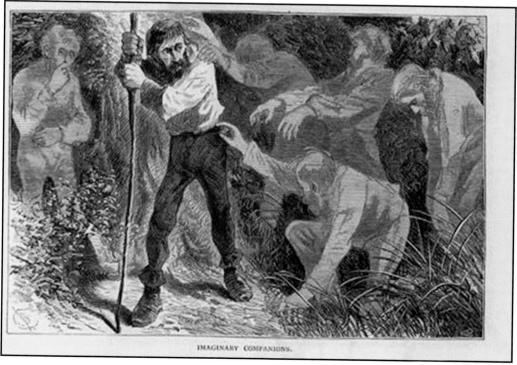

IMAGINARY COMPANIONS.

Weary and delusional, Everts believed he saw ghosts in Yellowstone.

Now his possessions were reduced to only a small knife and an opera glass. He huddled next to hot springs to survive the nights' freezing temperatures, but when he got too close to the boiling water, he was scalded. Cleverly, he used his opera glass to amplify the sun's rays and create a flame so he could build a warming fire. It was a tedious process, though, and in the end, Everts chose to carry a burning torch in one hand everywhere he went.

Attempts to find food often failed or left him sick. He grasped at a toad once, but it slipped through his fingers. When he gulped down a handful of raw minnows, they made him violently ill. The only reliable food source proved to be the fibrous roots of thistle plants, which Everts dug out of the ground with his hands and knife.

After a month had passed, most of the party had given up hope that Everts was still alive. In a last-ditch effort, they dispatched a local woodsman to find him. And, on the thirty-seventh day after Everts had gone missing, the woodsman, out roaming the Yellowstone landscape, spied what he thought was a wounded animal up ahead. A bear, he wondered?

Stepping in closer, he heard the creature groan. The limp and crumpled body, he realized, was that of a man.

His body was emaciated and battered, yet somehow Everts was still alive. One side of his body was blackened and blistered, as he'd accidentally burned himself while sleeping near hot springs. The bones on his feet were exposed. His fingers resembled a bird's claws. His rescuer carried Everts's limp, fifty-pound body back to camp.[38]

Months later, Everts was mostly recovered from his wounds. He even agreed to recount his terrifying ordeal for an article in *Scribner's Monthly*.

***

Roaring Mountain, a steaming, hissing hillside in Yellowstone.

Ultimately, the Langford-Washburn Expedition spent six weeks in Yellowstone. The combination of an early fall snowstorm, which dumped two feet of snow on the region, and dwindling food supplies hastened the group's departure. Yet, they all managed to survive, carrying home journals and notebooks filled with some of the most fantastic material to ever come out of the American West.

The problem was, few newspapers took the accounts seriously.

The same thing had happened a year earlier to three other Montanans who'd ventured into Yellowstone successfully and tried to have their accounts of the steaming landscape published. When one of the men submitted his story to a local paper, its editor responded, "Thank you, but we do not print fiction."[39] Larger papers and magazines, including the *New York Tribune, Scribner's,* and *Harper's,* also declined, stating that they couldn't risk their reputations on "such unreliable material."[40]

A year later, *Scribner's* changed its mind and decided that it couldn't turn down Langford's tantalizing piece on the Yellowstone region. A few of Langford's companions also managed to get their accounts published—mostly in local and regional papers.

The increasing publicity helped pique Americans' interest in the strange place known as Yellowstone. Langford's lectures—he was scheduled to do twenty of them across the country—also stoked public curiosity about the odd region out West.

But there was more to Langford's story than just sheer enthusiasm for natural and quirky wonders. In truth, he'd become entangled with one of the wealthiest men in 1870s America, a man who considered Yellowstone to be little more than the focus of his next publicity stunt.

★★★

Most Americans knew the name of Jay Cooke; in fact, "rich as Jay Cooke" was a popular expression.[41]

Well-known for his dapper dress, which often included a shiny top hat and sweeping black cape, Cooke was among the era's wealthiest men. It was a list that included some of the nation's biggest tycoons, including Andrew Carnegie, Jay Gould, and John D. Rockefeller.

Cooke's Philadelphia mansion was furnished with more than three hundred paintings and sculptures, and featured a "hunting room" and large theater. No sign of

Jay Cooke.

decadence was too much for Cooke. He even insisted that his Cuban cigars come wrapped in glass sleeves, each one etched with his initials.

Cooke made his fortune during the Civil War by selling thousands of government bonds to Union supporters. He deployed patriotic-sounding newspaper ads to help convince Americans to buy his bonds. Ruthlessly, he made his pitch to poor laborers who could hardly afford the bond, and to Quakers who outwardly opposed the war.[42]

Now Cooke had a new scheme brewing, one in which Yellowstone and its supposed wonders would play a pivotal part. The well-connected banker and salesman planned to punch a *second* transcontinental railroad across the United States.

There was no real demand for Cooke's Northern Pacific, as the nation had barely finished celebrating its first transcontinental line, which was completed in 1869. It had been a major feat: more than 1,900 miles of tracks had been excruciatingly laid by workers, many of whom perished in the effort.

With a colossal cross-country railroad already in existence, it made little sense to Americans why Cooke would build another, especially one that would slice

A Technological Marvel Built on Blood, Sweat, and Tears

The ambitious scheme to link the country's West and East Coasts via train officially kicked off when President Abraham Lincoln signed the Railroad Act of 1862. Americans hoped that a transcontinental railroad would unify the United States, a nation still engaged in a bitter Civil War. And given the era's rampant bigotry, there were also people who believed the United States was morally obliged to "civilize" the rugged frontier and "cleanse" it of its savage Natives and wild animals. They rallied the advent of large rumbling trains that would deliver white settlers and industry to the Great Plains and beyond, and displace American Indian tribes who'd inhabited the West for hundreds of years.

Many Americans in the mid-1800s called on "civilization" to tame the grotesque wilds of the West. The incoming railroads, cattle, and wagons full of white settlers ultimately displaced many American Indian tribes and wildlife.

The railroad tracks that sliced their way across the valleys, mountains, and deserts of the western frontier were constructed by laborers who suffered their own set of problems. Many were Irish and Chinese immigrants who had fled war or famine in their own countries and were willing to assume the most grueling of jobs—especially if it meant a chance for a fresh opportunity in America.

Railroad tracks slice through a Colorado canyon.

Railroad crews risked serious injury, even death, as they toiled for twelve hours a day, six days a week. They built bridges over raging rivers, carved roadbeds out of granite, and blasted away portions of mountains—the latter being the most dangerous work. Men were lowered down steep cliffs in small baskets to plant black powder inside rock crevices. While hanging there, they'd frantically light a fuse and toss it in the powder, praying that their fellow workers would pull them up and away from the fiery explosion in time.

In the end, America's transcontinental railroad was considered a colossal feat. It connected remote regions of a fast-growing country, allowing travelers to see portions of the continent they had previously only read about. The railroad was also vital to western expeditions, enabling explorers to transport the men, animals, and bulky supplies needed to carry out complex missions.

through the sparsely settled American Northwest. Cornelius Vanderbilt joked that it was "a railroad from nowhere, to nowhere."[43] But that didn't matter to Cooke. The plot, like so many others in the late 1800s, was simply a ploy to make a lot of money.

Yellowstone's part in the plan was to lure prospective train riders westward. What better way to sell railroad tickets than to tempt riders with a land teeming with incredible wonders?

With that goal in mind, Cooke and his publicity manager hatched the same lecture tour that brought Langford into contact with important politicians and civilians alike, with the added bonus that Cooke's politician friend, Congressman Blaine, would warmly introduce Langford to the crowd.

Ferdinand Hayden.

Public skepticism, however, continued to hamper Cooke's plan. Many Americans still doubted that a land teeming with boiling absurdities really existed. But one man sitting in the audience the night of Langford's Washington, DC, lecture had the power to lift the curtain on Yellowstone once and for all.

He was Ferdinand V. Hayden, one of the nation's leading geologists working in the American West.

This wasn't the first time Hayden had heard about the land of steaming waters. Ten years prior, he'd tried breaching the massive snowy walls around Yellowstone to see the wonders for himself. He'd been invited by the US Army Corps of Topographical Engineers to join an expedition into the region. During that time, the US army carried out all official explorations across the western frontier until the US Geological Survey was established in the 1860s.

Despite expert guidance from mountain man Jim Bridger, the party was hampered by a sudden spring blizzard and never got to see, as their army captain bemoaned, "the most interesting unexplored district in . . . our country."[44]

That didn't stop Hayden from trekking across the frontier and planning a possible return to Yellowstone. The intense man with pale blue eyes and brown side-swept hair had a passion for science, discovery, and the West. As both a naturalist and geologist, he spent years crisscrossing the Rocky Mountains and hunting for the strange and novel—whether it was dinosaur teeth or mastodon bones.

And now the time was ripe for the most novel adventure of all: an expedition into Yellowstone. As Hayden sat in the lecture hall listening to Langford, he plotted his next mission. Excited and determined as he was, Hayden had never organized an expedition as ambitious as the one he hoped to take to Yellowstone. He knew it was going to need a lot of planning—and an army of the nation's brightest and brawniest men.

Snowy peaks flanking the northeastern side of Yellowstone.

CHAPTER 3
GO WEST!

I could live as the wild Indian lives . . .[45]

—Ferdinand V. Hayden

Ferdinand Hayden had always been fascinated with the strange and beautiful.

Whether it was curiosities in nature or the pretty girlfriends he courted as a young man, beauty had long been a passion of Hayden's. He loved roaming the hills and woods in search of new sights. It was a way to escape life's struggles—and to forget his painful past.

Hayden was born in 1829 in a small town in Massachusetts to parents he would never really know. His father, an alcoholic who stumbled from one cockeyed money-making scheme to another, never supported the family.

That left Hayden's mother with the job of raising three children alone. But the task proved too burdensome for the young woman. Wishing to start a new life, she remarried, had a fourth child, and sent her two oldest children, one of whom was Hayden, off to live with relatives. Twelve-year-old Ferdinand was separated from his sister and sent to live in Ohio with an aunt he'd never met before.[46]

Ferdinand Hayden.

Hayden was a "sensitive and spirited child" who enjoyed flipping over rocks and learning the names of trees and plants.[47] He grew to be an inquisitive teenager who yearned to go to school to learn more about his natural surroundings. His aunt supported him, yet given her modest circumstances, she wasn't able to provide Hayden with the proper education the young man craved.

Desperate to leave his small farm town and to attend college, sixteen-year-old Hayden asked a wealthy uncle for help. The uncle valued education—his own daughter attended a reputable boarding school—but the only thing he offered Hayden was preachy advice. Obstacles help build character, he told Hayden in a letter. They help young people grow into "the most persevering and useful citizens."[48]

The determined Hayden found another way to get to the university. By teaching children at a local school and doing odd jobs such as cutting firewood, Hayden raised about half of the money necessary to attend nearby Oberlin College.[49] The school loaned him the remaining funds, and he enrolled in 1846.

At school Hayden pursued his passion but was often ridiculed for it. A professor belittled him for his interest in flowers—"common weeds," the man called them.[50] Hayden was an aimless wanderer, some of his classmates thought, "an enthusiastic dreamer who could never conquer in practical life."[51] He was "coarsely dressed, not overly clean," according to another peer, likely due to his hikes through muddy fields and woods.[52]

Regardless of his detractors, Hayden, or "Ferd" as his classmates called him, remained focused on his studies, especially the natural sciences. Books, poetry, and art also preoccupied him, as did flings with young women.

Of his many girlfriends, the closest was Hattie Brooks. She and Hayden had a special friendship; he could share his inner thoughts with her, something that serious men weren't encouraged to do. But even Hattie would tire of Hayden's dreaminess over time. She chided him for spending too much time "pouring over some foolish book."[53]

After graduating from Oberlin in 1850, Hayden—still interested in natural science—pursued the only advanced degree in that field he could at the time: medicine. In mid-nineteenth century America, advanced courses in fields like biology and botany didn't exist yet. So a medical degree was the next logical step for Hayden—training, he may not have realized, that would prove invaluable later. During his time in medical school, Hayden became acquainted with leading naturalists of the day, including geologist John Strong Newberry and paleontologists James Hall and Joseph Leidy. After graduating in 1853 from Albany Medical School in New York, Hayden implored his distinguished friends for an opportunity he'd long awaited: to join a geological collecting expedition in the American West.

Paleontologist Joseph Leidy.

***

Sketch of Hayden attracting insects to a flame.

Inquisitive and eager for outdoor adventure, some women also worked as naturalists and collectors in nineteenth-century America, including Martha Maxwell, pictured here.

For the next several years, Hayden trekked across portions of present-day Kansas, North Dakota, South Dakota, Wyoming, and Montana gathering thousands of rocks and fossils, as well as specimens of animals, birds, reptiles, insects, and plants.

Collections were an important tool for naturalists in the 1800s. They were a way to organize the planet's staggering array of life. Roaming across distant territories, collectors hammered away at rocks and dug up fossils. They dunked small animals and reptiles, still alive, into jars filled with alcohol, preserving them so they could be studied back in a laboratory. When supplies of pure alcohol ran out, collectors saved precious specimens in bottles of whiskey or rum; "the stronger the better," advised expert collector Spencer Baird of the Smithsonian Institution.[54] Collectors also skinned mammals and preserved the pelts by dusting them with powdered arsenic—a workplace hazard that caused headaches, nausea, and sometimes death. They captured unusual new insects during the night by luring them to the flame of a candle.

The uncharted American West was an especially fertile fossil bed. On one trip, Hayden dredged up the remains of several prehistoric creatures, including a mastodon, elephant, rhinoceros, and a camel, which would have been about one-third the size of the modern animal.[55]

Hayden found a close friend and professional ally in Spencer Baird. Probably

Spencer Fullerton Baird, Secretary of the Smithsonian Institution from 1878 to 1887.

A naturalist's or collector's field notes.

the most influential naturalist of his time, Baird helped Hayden secure choice collecting assignments. And soon, Hayden himself became a renowned collector.

The sheer size of Hayden's collection was impressive alone. One load he shipped back East weighed one thousand pounds. Over a period of only two years digging in the West, Hayden racked up the following finds:

77 fossil vertebrates
251 fossil mollusks
70 fossil plants
423 rock specimens
47 mammals
186 birds
65 mollusks
24 fishes
28 reptiles
1,500 plants[56]

Baird's sparrow, named for the famous nineteenth-century naturalist Spencer Baird.

As usual, the specimens were shuttled back East to be classified and described by various experts. Included in one particular haul were several curious black triangular bits.

Baird was stunned when he saw them. He quickly informed distinguished paleontologist Joseph Leidy of the discovery, telling him the fossils "will make your eyes water."[57] Leidy identified the pointy black bits as teeth belonging to some of the first dinosaurs found in America.

Of course, collector and naturalist work entailed many physical hardships, such as hunger, extreme weather, and violence waged by angered Native tribes. But none of that stopped Hayden from pursuing the thing he loved most. Once, when food supplies ran out on a collecting trip, he subsisted

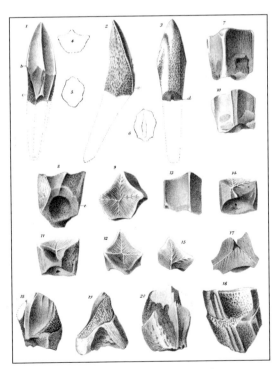

Sketches of dinosaur teeth (*Trachodon*) unearthed by Hayden.

for several days on scraps from a prairie dog. On another trip, he suffered temporary blindness and dehydration while navigating the bleached sand walls of the South Dakota Badlands.

Over the years, Hayden became accustomed to interacting with American Indian tribes. Generally, he came to respect the lands they held sacred, a lesson he learned the hard way.

Early in his career, he'd been digging in the Montana Territory, working to amass a nice collection to send to colleagues back East. Hayden stored his finds at his camp, leaving them behind while he set out for new discoveries. One day, upon returning to camp, he discovered that many of his collected bones and fossils were missing.

Hayden hadn't known, or hadn't bothered to find out, that he'd been excavating lands that belonged to the Flathead American Indians. Angered, the Natives had dumped a portion of Hayden's specimens in a nearby river—a retaliation that could have ended much worse for the geologist.[58]

Hayden (seated) talking with a colleague.

Another tribe, members of the Sioux, seemed amused by Hayden's rock collecting. They called him "The Man-Who-Picks-Up-Stones-Running," a nickname that stuck with Hayden for the rest of his career.[59]

The Civil War, which drained the nation's finances, temporarily put an end to most organized expeditions. But once the war was over, the country was more eager than ever to inventory the contents of its vast and alluring western frontier. By then, large numbers of settlers had already made the grueling journey west in covered wagons. Farmers, ranchers, and prospectors who relocated to the plains were anxious to learn about the weather patterns, waterways, mountains, and other aspects of their new home.

In 1867, Hayden was asked to head one of the nation's official western surveys: the US Geological Survey of the Territories. He now had the power and freedom to lead his own expeditions in the West. Hayden also was finding satisfaction in his personal life. For several months he'd been dating Emma Woodruff, a young merchant's daughter from Philadelphia. She supported his unusual career and interests, which sent him gallivanting for months at a time across the wild frontier. Soon, the two were engaged.

Over the next four years, Hayden commanded his own expeditions—also called surveys—across the western United States. At the conclusion of each one, he published detailed reports describing the region's geography, climate, and other qualities. Many Americans followed these documents, so Hayden made special efforts to make them relatable and easy to read. He often used flowery, poetic prose, which was popular among readers in the Victorian era.

A Nation's Brave and Willing Explorers

Once the costly Civil War had ended, the United States resumed the work of mapping and documenting the West's exotic and promising lands. It established several official expeditions, later known as the Great Western Surveys, to carry out this work.

Congress and the American people were eager for details about the distant territories—their topography, farming potential, and whether or not they contained precious minerals such as gold or silver. The nuggets and seams of gold being pried and blasted out of California in the 1840s and '50s had already sent droves of people from all over the world scrambling.

The men hired to lead these government surveys were clever, daring, and often risked life and limb to secure information to include in their reports. They scaled mountains, braved lashing river rapids, and trudged across 118-degree Fahrenheit deserts—often ending their days hungry, parched, and ragged. They dodged vengeful Natives, as well as dangerous highwaymen—gun-toting thieves who roved the West on horseback, hunting for travelers to prey upon.

Expedition leader Ferdinand Hayden faced many dangers, as did his colleagues. On one trip, geologist Clarence King, who helped map much of California's Sierra Nevada Mountains, was struck by lightning. The incident reportedly caused one half of his body to turn brown for a week. American southwest explorer John Wesley Powell suffered a major blow during his expedition down the Colorado River in 1869 when three of his men were killed by a party of hostile American Indians.

The government's western explorers were bold and inquisitive public servants who assumed great risk to introduce their country to its majestic scenery.

And by the spring of 1871, Hayden was on the brink of embarking on his largest expedition yet.

***

That spring the geologist received an impressive $40,000 dollar appropriation from Congress to explore the greater Yellowstone region.[60] As usual, the funds

John Wesley Powell.

Powell consulting with Tau-Gu, Paiute Chief.

required political wrangling and the influence of some of his powerful friends. The most important was Representative Henry L. Dawes, who sat on the powerful House Committee on Appropriations. This committee was comprised of congressmen who controlled the purse strings in Washington.

As for logistics and planning, Hayden had a great partner and assistant in James Stevenson, who'd been traveling with the geologist for about fifteen years. Stevenson managed all the tedious details that came with planning a major scientific foray into the wilderness.

A quiet man from Kentucky, Stevenson arranged the men's travel aboard the Union and Pacific railroads from cities back east, as well as the wagons, horses, and pack mules that would carry them the rest of the way. He hired staff—cooks, laborers, animal packers, and guides—who carried out the less glamorous tasks of the expedition. Stevenson also agonized over lists of supplies, foodstuffs, tents, and other equipment needed to sustain a party of thirty-two men in the wilderness for six weeks.

But Hayden was still left with the enormous task of selecting the best minds and bodies to help him lay open Yellowstone's secrets. The trip was more than just a rigorous scientific investigation: it would test the party's survival instincts.

Hayden told the men he hired to expect "rough times and rough people."[61] They would have to know how to saddle a horse, load a gun, and scrounge for food in the wide open country.

A well-armed group of Westerners. Hayden's expedition members were also expected to carry rifles and wear belts stocked with extra bullets.

With so many esteemed colleagues, Hayden staffed his survey with some of the country's smartest men. And a few were proven outdoorsmen, having served with Hayden on earlier trips. He recruited experts on mammals, birds, fish, insects, plants, and rocks. To make maps, he counted on close friend and experienced topographer, Anton Schonborn. A meteorologist in the group recorded all the weather they encountered.

Hayden also recruited some of his recent students, including twenty-one-year-old Albert Peale, who'd studied under Hayden when he was a professor at the University of Pennsylvania. Quiet and modest, Peale came from a long line of distinguished nature enthusiasts. His great-grandfather was the Revolutionary War artist Charles Willson Peale, who famously painted portraits of George Washington, Thomas Jefferson, and Benjamin Franklin. Charles Willson Peale had also established the nation's first natural history museum, the Peale Museum in Philadelphia. Peale's grandfather later managed the museum, and Peale's uncle, Titian Peale, was a well-known naturalist who'd roamed across South America and the South Pacific.

The politically savvy Hayden also recruited a few sons of congressmen for the trip—including Henry Dawes's son, Chester—as a way of thanking the legislators

Albert Peale.

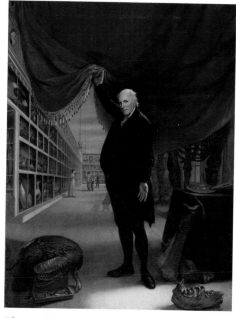

The *Artist in His Museum*, a self-portrait of naturalist Charles Willson Peale in his Philadelphia museum. Peale, great-grandfather of Hayden Expedition member Albert Peale, excited early Americans about science. His museum contained a menagerie of stuffed, pickled, and preserved natural wonders, including the wild turkey pictured in the foreground.

for their support. Hayden would use these men in supportive roles that didn't demand rigorous scientific know-how.

The scientists on Hayden's survey would need numerous tools: hammers for chipping at rocks, thermometers for dunking into pools, and barometers, pencils, and numerous field journals. There would be leaves to press, bird eggs to preserve in jars, and an array of small and large mammals to capture with guns, nets, or traps.

Spencer Baird, at the Smithsonian, also expected the team to return home with at least one perfect buffalo head. Scientists were running out of time to learn about this burly creature. It had once been so abundant in the West that its herds blackened the Great Plains, but now its population teetered on the edge of extinction—due in large part to the recent construction of the transcontinental railroad. Its tracks cut through the remote western prairies and valleys where the buffalo had long thrived. Hunters traveled on these trains and needed only to lean out of their railcar to fire at the animals. At the peak of buffalo hunting, an average of 120 buffalo were killed every forty minutes.

Science in the Field

Ferdinand Hayden, like other government-sponsored geologist-explorers, was expected to fill his official reports with reams of scientific data. The American public and Congress were hungry for information about their little-known western lands. People were curious: how tall were the West's mountains? How deep were its lakes? And in the case of Yellowstone: did spewing fountains really exist? Hayden and his crew needed to gather as much information as possible, using only the tools and crude technologies available in 1871.

Sextant.

Barometers, made of fragile glass that had to be carefully packed and handled, were used to measure elevations, including the height of mountains. Compasses were used to gauge direction and to map a party's course. Sextants, which measure the angle between two points, were used to compute latitude—a location's northerly or southerly position. This was often done by measuring the angle between a various point and the noonday sun when it is directly overhead.

Thermometers were of vital importance for measuring the temperatures of Yellowstone's simmering springs and mud pots. A basic geologist's hammer, which Hayden typically hung from his belt, was in constant use for chipping away at rock samples and examining their strata, or layers. The geologist also carried a small bottle of acid to help identify limestone, which would fizz and bubble if dribbled with the acid.

Given the limitations of these basic tools, the scientists were always improvising. They tasted cooled-off samples from hot springs to estimate acidity, and scientists memorized their bodies' exact dimensions—the height and the length of their arms, legs, and hands—so that they could use their own bodies as measuring rods.

***

Perhaps more important than science, however, was the art and imagery that Hayden hoped to bring back from the Yellowstone region. Through pictures and photos, he'd be able to provide Americans with the first tangible proof of the Land of Steaming Marvels.

Regardless of how colorfully he wrote, Hayden understood the limitations of words in conveying the majesty of America's western scenery. He wasn't the only one. As far back as 1805, Meriwether Lewis complained about the difficulty of describing nature without pictures. Once Lewis struggled to characterize a stunning waterfall, and the result, he wrote, left him "disgusted."[62]

Newspapers and magazines, as well as railroad promoters, benefited from artists' striking portrayals of landscapes. So, by the 1870s, photographers, painters, and sketch artists became regular participants in government and railroad surveys across the American West.

Expedition photographer hauling bulky supplies across the desert.

William Henry Jackson.

For Yellowstone, Hayden planned on having at least two artists in his group to capture the majesty of what they were about to explore. One was Henry Elliott, who'd worked for Hayden the previous year and had been drawing for the Smithsonian Institution since he was sixteen. He would be the human equivalent of a camera, transferring onto paper the widely ranging topography of Yellowstone: the sweeping lines of valleys and plains, and the jagged teeth of volcanic peaks.

The other artist Hayden knew personally: it was his friend, western photographer William H. Jackson. Jackson had worked with Hayden the previous summer, and his black-and-white photographs were used by railroad companies to decorate their brochures and posters.

But on this expedition, Jackson was poised to do something even more extraordinary: to bring back the first-ever photographs of the wild Yellowstone country.

CHAPTER 4
CHANGE IN PLANS

Many hardships lie before us, but we enter upon our work with stout hearts and great interest.

　　　　　—Robert Adams, Jr., member of Hayden's 1871 Yellowstone expedition

FORT ELLIS, MONTANA TERRITORY, JULY 1871

A baseball whizzed through the pine-infused air. In a stadium of open sky and snow-plastered peaks, a group of men abandoned their worries—at least for the moment.

After months of planning, Ferdinand Hayden's Yellowstone expedition was nearing its destination. Hayden and his thirty-two men had arrived at Fort Ellis, an army post in the Montana Territory. Here, they would load up on final supplies and recruit additional horses and mules needed for hauling their massive load into the wilderness.

For most of the group, the journey started almost two months prior when

Fort Ellis, Montana Territory, 1871.

they boarded trains in Chicago, Philadelphia, and Washington, DC. They had scrambled on and off connecting lines until reaching Ogden, Utah—the closest rail stop to the Yellowstone region at the time.

It had been an arduous trip. The hard wooden seats and the jolting movements of the train made the travelers' bones rattle. They suffered through insomnia, motion sickness, and bad food. The stench of garlic and unbathed bodies filled the train's cramped spaces, only alleviated by the sharp smell of tobacco.

But rewards came when the men gazed out the greasy train windows. By the time the expedition group reached the huge sweep of the Great Plains, the sky

A train passenger's perspective.
Photo by William Henry Jackson.

widened and the scenery unfolded. As the train whistle blared, they rumbled by serpentine rivers, rolling valleys, and white-capped mountain peaks.

In addition to the scenery, the travelers were struck by the new settlements cropping up along the railroad line. George Allen, Hayden's former geology professor at Oberlin, observed: "Towns are springing up everywhere as if by magic."[63] He also noticed "bleached skulls and skeletons," the remains of buffalo scattered along the sides of the rails.[64]

When the party stepped off the train platform in Ogden, Utah, it was time to round up the horses and pack mules—fifty animals in total—that would deliver the men and all their provisions north to the Montana Territory. Led by Hayden, the party traveled together. Little did they know that they would soon meet some of the West's harshest elements.

Hayden expedition team at camp.

The winding train of men and animals endured 105 degree temperatures as they crossed the dry, sage-covered flats of today's Idaho. The animals' hooves kicked up clouds of dust that made the men cough and their eyes burn. In the evening, at creek-side campsites, mosquitoes swarmed so thickly that the men slept with netting draped over their faces.

From the start, the scientists worked to record all the natural curiosities around them in their field journals. One of their first significant sightings was a large rattlesnake, whose tail, they discovered upon dissecting, contained fourteen rattles.[65]

They continued their march north, stopping in Virginia City in the Montana Territory, the site of a once-bustling gold mine. They saw gouged hillsides and twenty-foot-tall piles of dredged earth, but most of the gold chasers themselves had gone. These men had already stripped the land of most of its glitter. Now just a few Chinese gold seekers remained, allowed only to comb through the rubble that others had abandoned.

Virginia City, Montana Territory, 1871.

Before leaving Virginia City, Hayden's party enjoyed the last hot, satisfying meal they'd have for almost two months: oyster stew and steak. Then they climbed back in their saddles and continued on the bumpy, dusty stagecoach road to Fort Ellis, their last major stop before heading into Yellowstone territory.

With packing chores completed, many in the party seized upon some much-needed downtime. Near mountain meadows speckled with bright wildflowers, a group of Hayden's men played baseball with soldiers from the fort. As they hooped and hollered, forgetting the stressful travel of the last few weeks, their leader was preoccupied with distressing news. An army officer informed Hayden that violence was increasing in the Yellowstone Valley. Hayden should prepare his party for an attack by a hostile tribe.

Conflicts between whites and American Indians over gold and other resources had been escalating in the last decade. But now a new irritant had emerged, and local Sioux people were angry.

The source of the trouble: Jay Cooke's Northern Pacific railroad. In their hunt for prime real estate, Cooke's railroad surveyors were trespassing on lands in the Montana Territory that belonged to the Sioux. There was a good chance the tribe would retaliate, but it wasn't yet clear how or when.

Cooke already had access to a large swath of land, as had the owners of the other big railroads, the Union Pacific and Central Pacific. Over the years, these companies had successfully lobbied Congress into giving them millions of acres worth of land grants.

During lavish lunches and in hushed backroom deals, powerful railroad men often bribed members of Congress. They promised politicians shares of railroad stock and other gifts in exchange for votes that benefited the railroads. Because of their corrupt tactics, the railroad barons became known as "robber barons" by their critics in the popular press. Ultimately, Cooke would amass the largest land prize given to any US railroad—a size equivalent to all of New England.[66]

Hayden's 1871 expedition team.

Those lands came primarily from two sources: Native peoples' lands and public domain lands—lands that, in theory, belonged to all Americans.

Given the recent news, the army officer at Fort Ellis advised Hayden to take at least forty soldiers with him on his expedition through Yellowstone. That meant his party would number about seventy men in total.

It seemed a major burden to Hayden—managing the additional men, as well as the necessary food, provisions, and logistics they would require. Even before this news arrived, Hayden had worried that his party was too large. "I am now overwhelmed and fearful," he confided to his former professor George Allen in a letter months earlier, "lest I cannot pull through with what I have."[67]

In addition, Hayden had already prepared his party for potential scuffles with local American Indians. Each man carried a gun strapped across his shoulders and wore a belt full of extra bullets. They also carried knives, spurs, and whips, looking, as Albert Peale later noted, "quite formidable."[68]

In the end, however, Hayden had no choice but to accept a military escort. He couldn't risk the welfare of his men—or his mission.

★★★

As the group set out toward Yellowstone, Hayden adjusted to more unexpected news. He learned that George Allen, his former professor and the most experienced geologist on the expedition, was leaving within days. The stress was just too much for the fifty-eight-year-old man, who found camp life barbaric and the threat of American Indian attacks too unnerving. This meant that Hayden's former student, Albert Peale, would have to assume one of the most critical positions of the survey. The young man had never traveled West before, but he was eager for adventure and to please the man he called "Doctor."

Hayden also learned of *another* addition to his group. In Virginia City, he'd received a curious letter from a traveling stagecoach. The sender asked the following question: Would Hayden consider taking another man on his trip—an artist, the letter said, of "rare genius"?

The letterhead read JAY COOKE AND COMPANY.[69]

Thomas Moran.

The artist, it turned out, was the one assigned to illustrate Langford's *Scribner's* article. His name was Thomas Moran. Moran was a struggling artist from England who aspired to be a landscape painter but who meanwhile made his living and supported his family as a woodblock artist. Woodblocks were a common way to print large numbers of illustrations in the nineteenth century. They were made by carving a relief of the desired image onto a hard block of wood using a sharp awl-like tool. The remaining surface was then brushed with ink and pressed onto paper.

Cooke had likely seen Moran's work in the recent *Scribner's* article and figured it would make a nice addition to his own Yellowstone campaign. So his publicity manager appealed to *Scribner's* editors in New York to see if Moran might be interested in joining the summer's much-acclaimed Yellowstone expedition. And as Cooke also had to convince Hayden of the arrangement, his team enticed the expedition leader with the cryptic telegram, offering the services of an artist of "rare genius." Moran, it turned out, was more than eager to join the expedition, since he yearned to see and paint the vast scenery of America's West; especially the wondrous region that he'd earlier been asked to illustrate. It couldn't have been a better deal for the Northern Pacific: the railroad got an artist into Yellowstone at little cost to itself, and would soon secure dazzling images for its publicity campaign.

Thomas Moran's woodcut of a geyser appearing in *Scribner's Monthly.*

The railroad might have guessed that Hayden would

Erin Peabody

also be delighted to have Moran join the expedition. The geologist-explorer knew the importance of artists: they helped to illustrate his fieldwork, and demonstrated the value of his government-funded work. So now, Hayden would have three artists to help him document the exciting phenomenon ahead: Henry Elliott for sketching, William H. Jackson for photographs, and Thomas Moran for bringing rich color to the imagery through his watercolors and paintings.

Putting Mountains on Canvas

German-born Albert Bierstadt, who moved to America as a small child, was an established western artist at the time of Hayden's 1871 expedition. Hayden had hoped Bierstadt would join him in documenting Yellowstone's wonders, but the artist ended up making other plans—a choice that would ultimately launch Thomas Moran's career. Having traveled with other western explorers, Bierstadt had already seen much of the American West, including the craggy peaks of the Rocky Mountains.

Albert Bierstadt.

Inspired by what he'd seen there, Bierstadt returned to the East and created a monumental and breathtaking piece—a painting that gave Americans one of their first glimpses of the West's majestic scenery.

The oil painting, revealed in the spring of 1863, was immense. It stretched ten feet long and featured snow-marbled mountains towering over a valley. It was so lifelike and grand that viewers could have imagined standing alongside Bierstadt as he first beheld the striking scene.

The painting's scale and subject matter wowed the public and art lovers. *The Rocky Mountains, Lander's Peak*, as it was titled, ultimately fetched $25,000—then the highest sum ever awarded an American artist.

***

When Moran strolled into camp near Virginia City, he carried with him only a carpetbag and his sketching materials. The thirty-four-year-old man, with a trailing gray beard and light eyes, had risked a lot to get there. The artist, with a family back East to support, had no money to splurge on the cross-country adventure. Jay Cooke and Co. covered a portion of his travel costs. He also received a $500 loan from *Scribner's*, but only after he offered as collateral one of his most cherished possessions: a well-praised painting of a magical woodland scene.

What motivated Moran to take the job was a chance to see the West's spectacular scenery, images of which were increasingly popping up in magazines and travel books. He admired the works of Albert Bierstadt, whose glowing canvases of mountain peaks and skies were already causing a sensation back East. Further, it was the chance to visit a place that he'd only before imagined. He had struggled, in his work on the *Scribner's* article, to fathom the bizarre wonders that Langford described: the mud volcanoes, shooting fountains, terrible canyons.

Moran wanted to see it all, yet the "greenhorn," as he called himself, was brand new to the West.[70] He'd never ridden a horse and, until just a few days prior, had never experienced the jarring, sometimes terrifying ride aboard a stagecoach. Stagecoaches shuttled customers between frontier towns that were not yet served by rail lines.

Crammed with customers sweating in the dry heat, western stagecoaches jerked riders along poorly maintained roads, stirring up clouds of dust that invaded passengers' eyes and noses, and coated their lips and teeth. The biggest concern, however, was the threat of gunfire. Because many coaches carried gold and large amounts of cash, they became major targets for highway robbers and other bandits. Therefore, most stagecoaches were heavily armed, usually by a large man sitting "shotgun"—the origin of the term—next to the driver.

Moran rode the stagecoach for 350 miles, a ride that

The Rocky Mountains, Landers Peak, by Albert Bierstadt.

Western stagecoach.

lasted four days and four nights. By the end of the trip, he was drained, and his nerves were frayed. Stagecoach travel, as another passenger once described it, "reduces the traveler to a state bordering on insanity."[71] But Moran managed to arrive safely in Virginia City, and was greeted enthusiastically by Hayden. Soon, the Englishman would lay eyes on the steaming spectacles that earlier he could only picture in his mind.

✳✳✳

By now, Hayden's whole company, including the extra soldiers and additional pack animals, was ready to depart Fort Ellis. Hayden had also hired a local woodsman, a Mexican known only as Jose. His job was to help guide the group across the little-known Yellowstone country and, as their hunter, to supply the team with fresh meat. Dried goods, including flour, bacon, prunes, and coffee, were carried in smaller quantities: too hefty a load would be a burden to the animals as they trudged over rugged terrain.

On the morning of July 15, the noisy parade of animals and riders struck out along the emerald-green Yellowstone River. The mules were loaded

Hayden expedition hunters, including Jose.

Base Station

The Hayden Expedition established a base camp at Bottler's Ranch, just north of the Yellowstone region. The rustic cabin, built in 1868 by a pair of Dutch immigrants, served primarily as a stopover for hunters and prospectors on their way into the Yellowstone country.

Albert Peale seated on a fence at Bottler's Ranch.

Hayden posted a few of his less technically skilled hires here to deliver and collect mail from a nearby post. Other members of the party, including Hayden's chief assistant Stevenson, journeyed between Bottler's Ranch and locations across Yellowstone to keep the party stocked up on food, supplies, and medicine.

But most of the men equated Bottler's Ranch with the delicacy of fresh buttermilk. Before heading south into Yellowstone, Albert Peale wrote in his journal about enjoying his last cup of milk for several weeks. Perishable foods, like dairy, were never carried on expeditions into the wilderness as they were prone to spoilage. Instead, dried and preserved foods—including prunes, cured pork, and flour for biscuits—were staples the men would consume daily.

with tents, blankets, tools, pots, pans, and foodstuff. Jingling as they went, the pack train reminded a later journalist on a Yellowstone expedition of a "traveling country store."[72]

Each man was weighted down, too, with heavy coats, guns, ammunition, and tools, such as knives and hammers. Saddlebags were stuffed with clothing, towels, and bars of soap. Woolen blankets, the men's only bedding in the wild, were either draped under saddles or rolled up behind them as they rode.

Eventually, the more established wagon roads disappeared and the ride became rough for Hayden's group. There were bumps, ruts, and whole boulders that had to be dislodged so that the horse carts could pass.

The men soon spied linear drag marks on the ground, a sign that they were now traveling on American Indian trails. The marks were made by the Crow people,

The Yellowstone Range from Near Fort Ellis, by Thomas Moran.

who dragged their teepee poles behind them in their migrations between hunting grounds.

Hayden's group gazed at mountains to their east that reminded Hayden of "gigantic pyramids."[73] Pungent sagebrush prickled the men's noses like a chest salve.

Yet for every stunning scene, there seemed to be a setback. As they climbed higher into the mountains, the trail grew steeper and rockier. Their animals hugged the inner walls of mountain passes that dropped off precipitously. Once, as the team struggled to pull the roped animals up the hill, a pack mule suddenly tumbled over a cliff. The horse cart carrying foodstuffs and supplies almost toppled as they crept through a precarious canyon.

The strange land, however, lured them on. The landscape grew different; black shards of glassy rock, embedded in boulders and cliffs, shone in the sun. The animals' hooves clattered over ground that sounded hollow.

As the team wound around the next hill, they glimpsed large clouds of steam. They now stood on the brink of the much-fabled Wonderland, and awaiting them, as Peale would later describe, was "one of the grandest sights imaginable."[74]

CHAPTER 5
A MAMMOTH SIGHT

We can hear the water seething and boiling below like a cauldron . . .
—Ferdinand Hayden, from his "Fifth Annual Report of Progress,"
the official government report on Yellowstone[75]

A gleaming white mountain rose before Hayden's group. Vapors swirled from its summit and filled the sky. The men dashed in for a closer look. Terraces wound up the face of the mountain, resembling frozen stairs. "Like some vast frozen cascade," observed an astonished Peale.[76] After the group dismounted and secured their horses, the men scampered up the white terraces to explore.

Waters rushed down the mountain's scalloped edges and collected in pools. The pools bubbled gently, decorated with pearl-like stones. Stalactites hung like rows of icicles.

The survey's two geologists, Hayden and Peale, climbed carefully up the terraces. Not all were white, they noticed; some dripped with a gelatinous peach, orange, and brown substance. Hayden stared into a pool that was so clear and calm, he wrote, that one could see "the smallest cloud that flits across it."[77]

White Mountain, or today's Mammoth Hot Springs.

The huge ivory sculpture towered six hundred feet above their heads, and its waters burbled gracefully. But this "icy" mountain was not at all what it seemed.

In truth, many of its pools measured 160 degrees Fahrenheit or hotter and could have scalded a man. And when Hayden and the others stepped in for a closer look, they were engulfed in foul-smelling vapors saturated with sulfur.

Mammoth Hot Springs: A Mountain in Motion

The gleaming white rock that constitutes the bulk of Mammoth Hot Springs (what the Hayden Expedition called White Mountain) is a substance called travertine. It's produced when the bedrock in the area—limestone—gets cooked by the boiling waters burbling up from beneath it. This heat reduces the rock to a mineral-rich solution.

As that solution rushes, trickles, and drips, it hardens into a variety of forms—from large cauliflower-looking mounds to stalactites to pearl-like beads. The travertine terraces and their peculiar deposits are constantly changing, which makes Mammoth Hot Springs the most dynamic geologic wonder in Yellowstone.

Today's Canary Spring, at Mammoth Hot Springs.

This hill, adorned with snow-white baubles, had not been forged by ice. Rather, it was created by fire. Hayden and Peale could not have known it, but only a few miles beneath their boots a molten, red-hot furnace smoldered.

***

The next day, a figure crouched beside one of the color-stained pools. Underneath a floppy hat, a pair of eyes focused intently on the soft shades of the stone and water. It was the painter, Thomas Moran, studying Diana's Bath, the name the party gave to the hot spring.

Ever since he was a young boy, Moran knew he wanted to paint. His goal, he told school friends, was to make the pictures that appeared on banknotes. Not everyone understood his budding passion, however. Once, as a young teen, he slipped into a local gallery to admire the pictures just to have a staff member shoo him away, leaving him too humiliated to return.[78]

Still, Moran, described once as "the gentlest, noblest spirit," continued to draw, paint, and study the work of artists he admired.[79] And there was a new cadre of artists he was especially enthralled with: the landscape painters. These pioneers had no use for the gentle pastoral settings that featured red barns, grazing cows, and fences. The

Thomas Moran atop White Mountain.

natural world they wanted to capture on canvas was raw, wild, and free.

Humans started disappearing as subjects in the landscape painters' canvases. Paintings that once depicted plows raking the earth and trains slicing through fleeing herds of buffalo gave way, instead, to scenes that revealed glowing hills and sweeping mountains, devoid of any human mark. Some artists deliberately left out signs of civilization so that audiences could focus more intently on nature itself.

This group of landscape artists, to which Moran would eventually belong, was known as the Hudson River School. Most were based in New York City, due to its thriving art scene, but they regularly ventured out to the forests and streams of the nearby Hudson River Valley for inspiration.

How freeing it must have been to escape the drudgery of studio work! For so long American artists had been instructed to mimic the European masters and paint, day after day, the same still lifes, portraits, and ancient ruins that had been copied hundreds of times before.

As Moran took in the steaming landscape with its bizarre architecture, he realized how much the initial sketches he'd made for *Scribner's* paled in comparison to the real thing. They fell far "short of the vast fantastic freaks of nature," he wrote later.[80]

★★★

Not far from Moran, another artist labored to capture the scenery. It was photographer William H. Jackson, who had much more equipment to carry than just a sketchbook and pencils. Helping Jackson was his faithful beast of burden,

Pioneer photographer William H. Jackson packing a heavy load.

Hypo. This "fat little mule with cropped ears" he once wrote, is "as indispensable to me as his namesake, hyposulphite of soda."[81] Hypo, named after one of the chemicals needed to make nineteenth-century pictures, hauled Jackson's roughly three-hundred pounds of equipment. There were glass plates of numerous sizes, jugs of fresh water for rinsing the plates, and an array of chemicals used in developing black-and-white pictures.

"We may have looked as if we were ready for a picnic," Jackson later wrote, "but it wasn't one."[82] However, Jackson did discover a resource at White Mountain that made his job easier. "By washing the plates in water that issued from the springs at 160 degrees Fahrenheit, we were able to cut the drying time more than half."[83]

Jackson moved around the terraces searching for different perspectives to capture through his camera lens. He asked Moran to climb the terraces and pose, so that the people later viewing the picture would have a sense of the mountain's mammoth size. The two artists would continue to work closely throughout the expedition, sharing ideas and becoming lifelong friends.

★★★

Peale, meanwhile, crept along White Mountain's terraces. He jotted down figures, numbers, and descriptions into his notebook. He plunged a thermometer into dozens of hot pools and recorded their temperatures.

The young scientist was learning how to improvise in the field. When he couldn't gauge the mineral contents in one of the cooler springs, he

Trees often perish in the hot springs' steaming waters

scooped up a handful of the water and swished it in his mouth. "Slightly alkaline," he scribbled in his notebook.[84]

Peale shared Hayden's love for geology and, like him, could quickly become absorbed in the tedious work of peeling back rock layers, one careful chip at a time. He was rather quiet—a "nice little fellow," Hayden told Spencer Baird back at the Smithsonian.[85]

To help publicize the expedition and to keep curious Americans informed of their progress, Hayden asked Peale to write a series of articles for the *Philadelphia Press*, Peale's hometown paper. Hayden thought a newcomer to the West would provide a fresh and lively perspective to the group's expedition. Peale squeezed in time to write in the evenings, often by the light of a campfire, and used a slab of White Mountain's rock as a writing desk.

As for Hayden, he was busy exploring the hills behind White Mountain. A herd of antelope scattered as his boots crunched along the bleached layers of rock. He could see that steaming waters used to run here, but not anymore. Instead, gray weathered rocks lay jumbled in silent piles, reminding him of the ruins of "a once flourishing village."[86]

A pronghorn grazes on sagebrush.

Hayden, with his boy-like wonder, was enthralled by all the curiosities surrounding him. But there was no escaping the pressures that accompanied this well-publicized adventure. Politics played a big role in nineteenth-century western exploration and demanded that Hayden impress members of Congress with his survey's achievements. The more pleased the legislators were with his reports, the more money, he hoped, they would dole out for his future geological surveys.

Not only that, but Hayden wasn't the only one vying for the coveted funds. Three other illustrious explorers rivaled him for the government's money, as well as for the prestige and fame that came with western expeditions. One of the other government-funded explorers was hero John Wesley Powell, who'd recently braved the lashing rapids of the Colorado River with only one arm; he'd lost the other in the Civil War.

Clarence King, western explorer and geologist.

Hayden's most fierce competitor, however, was Clarence King, a Yale graduate who came from an influential family in New England. King was charming, well liked, and had already captured the public's attention with his poetic newspaper articles about California's Yosemite Valley.

Hayden—who grew up poor and abandoned by his mother and alcoholic father—desperately craved praise and recognition in his career. He hid his humiliating past from even his closest colleagues, inventing other stories about his upbringing to keep the truth from being exposed. A successful Yellowstone expedition, he hoped, would finally grant him the dignity he desired as an explorer and as a man.

As he climbed the ruins of White Mountain, Hayden discovered a large fissure in the Earth. He lowered himself inside the crack and realized the space opened into a dark underground cavern filled with sticks and animal bones. A swarm of bats flew past his face. There was a danger lurking here that the geologist did not expect: silent and invisible deadly gas.

An early tourist climbing inside an extinct Yellowstone hot spring, an area now closed due to dangerous levels of carbon dioxide.

Many of Yellowstone's hot springs and steaming vents ooze carbon dioxide and sulfur dioxide. Usually, these toxic gas molecules disperse with the wind. But in the case of underground caves or sinkholes—extinct hot springs—these poisonous gases can concentrate in deadly amounts, ready to steal their next victim's last breath.

Fortunately, Hayden didn't linger in the cavern for long. He hurried back to camp where a bonfire was crackling and many men were soaking in natural luxury; bone-chilled and saddle-sore, they couldn't resist slipping into Yellowstone's natural hot tubs. As the waters rush down the face of White Mountain, they cool and form pools with a variety of different temperatures, including some just right for a bath.

Rigors of Camp Life

While expedition work was filled with excitement and adventure, the realities of day-to-day living in the wilderness were often mundane and sometimes brutal. Sudden weather changes, food shortages, and concerns over hostile Native tribes were the most common challenges exploring parties faced.

Team discussing the day's plans at breakfast. Hayden is seated front left with assistant James Stevenson beside him.

But it was often the smallest of nuisances that drove men crazy. Mosquitoes swarmed camp and buzzed in the men's faces as they tried to eat, drink, and sleep. One expedition member was so covered with bites that he looked, he wrote later, as if he were stricken with measles. The parties' only defenses were to burn smoking fires made from buffalo chips (dung) and drape their faces with netting.

Homesickness also wore on the men. They wrote to their families and loved ones as often as they could and awaited letters that required weeks of postal travel across the wide open plains. Albert Peale, for instance, didn't learn about his uncle's death until several weeks after the man had died.

Hayden survey members enjoying some rare downtime.

Regardless, expedition members made the most of their frontier experience. They formed close bonds with their camp mates. They joked, played cards, and enjoyed the occasional cigar. And, according to expedition member Robert Adams, Jr., the party, at least once, savored ice-cold whiskey in the snowfields of Yellowstone's mountains: "Snowballs saturated with 'firewater,'" Adams reported, "is refreshing under a July sun."[87]

Today's Palette Spring, at Mammoth Hot Springs.

However, Hayden's party was surprised to find others soaking in the steam, too: several white men were clustered around mineral-laden pools nearby. They raved about the water's curative powers, which they said were good for treating arthritis as well as syphilis, a sexually transmitted disease that was common on the frontier. Not too far from Hayden's group's camp, they had a permanent camp built, with tents and wooden shacks.

Apparently, a booming enterprise was underway: a tourist resort that would sprawl across White Mountain. Two hopeful profiteers, J. C. McCartney and H. R. Horr, had struck out in their search for Montana gold, but when they heard about Yellowstone's hot silky waters, they knew that they'd discovered another kind of jackpot.

The men had just submitted a claim to 320 acres, all of White Mountain and its assortment of bubbling pools.[88] Jay Cooke's railroad would fit perfectly into their plan, as railcars could deliver flocks of new customers to their resort. It would prove to be a gold mine of another kind—one that threatened to destroy White Mountain's natural beauty forever. Little did Hayden know that he'd be battling these men's efforts in the months to come.

CHAPTER 6
TUMBLING WATERS

Nothing can be more chastely beautiful than this lovely cascade . . .
—Lieutenant Gustavus Doane, a member of the 1870 Langford-Washburn
party describing one of Yellowstone's many waterfalls

It was 4:00 a.m. when Peale jostled awake the two men replacing him for guard duty.

Each night, one or two men sat by the crackling fire and watched over the camp. Despite their exhaustion, they'd strain their tired bodies to stay awake, keeping an ear out for any slight stirring in the darkness. A prowling bear or mountain lion might spook the horses and mules and send them bolting. But even more importantly, the guard listened for the stealthy creep of angered Natives, who were most likely to ambush the group in the hours just before dawn.

After stealing an hour of sleep, Peale was up again, helping Hayden wrap glass bottles with scraps of cloth. The bottles contained samples of water cupped from White Mountain's pools, and like the other specimens—plant leaves, rock crumbles, bones, stuffed birds, and jars full of preserved animals, fish, and reptile parts—had to be packed carefully into wooden boxes. They needed to survive the grueling journey ahead—via mule, wagon, and later train—if they were going to serve as proof of Yellowstone's bizarre wonders.

Nighttime under Yellowstone skies.

It was mid-morning now, and with chores completed, the train of animals and men struck out to explore fresh country. They crossed swiftly moving creeks so

Arrowleaf balsamroot wildflower.

Indian paintbrush wildflower.

deep that the water rushed past the horses' chins. The team stopped to tighten saddles and loosen gear, then continued on, with the steaming terraces of White Mountain at their backs.

The horses plodded through tall grasses speckled with yellow, pink, purple, and red. Even though it was July, the spring season had just arrived in the mountains of Yellowstone. With snows mostly melted, wildflowers with names like Indian paintbrush, elephant head, and yellow monkeyflower soaked up the sun.

Expedition members pitching tents.

According to Hayden, the group was about to enter a "region of wonderful ravines and canyons."[89] The geologist had carefully read all the accounts from last year's Langford-Washburn Expedition, and anticipated some of what was to come.

The combination of deep crevices, canyons, and the streams that flow all over Yellowstone meant that the group would encounter breathtaking waterfalls. One of the first they saw rushed down a slope covered in ledges of dark brown rock. Peale noticed how

Land of Falling Waters

Tower Falls is just one of hundreds of waterfalls located in Yellowstone. And given the region's vast size and countless remote pockets, waterfalls are still being discovered in the area today.

Some of these waterfalls trickle over cliffs in long silvery threads. Others crash down ravines, thundering so loudly that all other sounds are snuffed out. Massive clouds of mist billow around many of them.

Waterfalls are categorized into two main types: a *waterfall*, which is a classic column of water plunging straight down; and a *cascade*, which tumbles down at an angle, usually over a series of mounded rocks.

Fairy Falls.

The names of Yellowstone's waterfalls, such as Fairy, Mystic, Osprey, and Moose, suit their far-ranging diversity. Kepler Cascades, for instance, was named after the twelve-year-old son of the governor of the Wyoming Territory, who toured Yellowstone in 1881.

the water bristled over the ledges and foamed, making the whole waterfall "look like snow from a distance."[90]

After a ride of eight or ten miles, the men stopped for camp and got busy with chores. They pitched their three fly tents under the cover of trees. The men shared these or slept out in the open air, using a saddle as a pillow. Jose, their guide and hunter, took whatever space was left, sometimes sleeping at the base of the tents.

Hayden occupied a larger tent that also stored all of his scientific papers and notebooks. He would often work late into the night, scribbling down geological notes and other observations made over the course of the day.

No man was more busy at camp, though, than "Potato John." John Raymond was head cook for the team and had served with Hayden before. He got his nickname from mistakenly serving hard, undercooked spuds to the men on one of Hayden's earlier expeditions. He hadn't realized that in the higher altitudes of

Hayden survey team enjoying a noon meal. Note camp cook "Potato John" Raymond on far left and photographer William H. Jackson on far right. Photo by William H. Jackson.

the mountains, water boils at lower temperatures, and so food requires longer cooking. Raymond soon adopted an easier method: he fried the potatoes instead, though the nickname stuck.

***

Something or someone spooked the animals that night. The horses and mules stampeded twice. The men scattered, too, in their mad hunt to round the animals up. No one knew what had startled the animals until the party packed up and left the next morning.

As they started down the trail, the men passed several large piles of wild animal droppings. "Bruin!" some shouted. It was obvious now that last night's intruder had been a grizzly.

In the late spring in Yellowstone, the humpbacked bears leave their dens to hunt for deer and elk weakened by the harsh winter. Later in the summer, the omnivores feast on mammals, trout, berries, seeds, nuts, and ants and termites that they rummage out of decaying logs.

A Top Predator Running Out of Space

Weighing between 250 and 600 pounds, grizzly bears are Yellowstone's largest predator. While they'll feed on weaker prey, including young elk calves and sickened animals, grizzlies eat a rich and varied diet that closely resembles our own. With their exceptional sense of smell—more powerful than even a hound dog's—the bears can track down a farmer's market of seasonal foods in Yellowstone's wilderness.

Wild strawberry.

In early spring, grizzlies feed on the carcasses of animals killed by harsh winter conditions, but also eat fresh dandelion greens, pine nuts, and ants. Later in the season, they swipe their three- to four-inch claws at the bright pink trout spawning in and around Yellowstone Lake. In summer they seek out the season's sweet smorgasbord of strawberries, huckleberries, whortleberries, and

Grizzly bears have an omnivorous diet that's much like our own.

buffalo berries. In fall, pine nuts provide an important source of fat that sustains the bears through their winter hibernation.

Pregnant females will typically give birth to two, three, or occasionally four cubs while in their winter den. Curious and playful, the cubs remain with their mother for at least two years.

Grizzlies are fascinating creatures that require thousands of square miles of wild habitat to find food and mates. While they used to roam freely across most of the western United States, Yellowstone remains one of the last places in the country where visitors still have the chance of seeing a grizzly bear.

The men rode on. They followed a creek that ran through a canyon that Hayden described as "deep and gloomy."[91] Then a roaring filled their ears. The party reached the spot where the creek hurled itself over a cliff. They'd have to climb deep inside the dark gorge if they were to see the thundering waterfall in full view. After tying up their horses at the top of the falls, they crept down the almost -vertical walls to the bottom, slipping and sliding much of the way.

After the heart-pounding descent, Hayden gazed up to the brink of the falls. On either side of the gushing water, huge steeples of rock rose toward the sky. They reminded Hayden of the "gigantic pillars at the entrance of some grand temple."[92] Last summer Langford's party had also been inspired by ancient architecture when they named the waterfall Tower Falls.

Meanwhile, Peale bolted upright in an ice-cold spray. He stood face-to-face with the falls now and was trying to gauge their width. They were twenty feet across, he approximated. And their height—about 160 feet.[93]

In his suspenders and bowler hat, Jackson, the photographer, looked vexed as he stared inside the deep crevice. It would be impossible, he thought, to carry his makeshift darkroom down those coarse and steep cliffs. How was he to capture a full-length picture of the falls? It proved to be, he later recalled, his "biggest photographic problem of the year."[94]

Developing photographs in the 1870s was like conducting a chemistry experiment with a stopwatch ticking. The approach Jackson used was called the "wet-plate process," since the glass plate, which became a photo in the end, had to be flushed with liquid chemicals. These coatings had to remain wet until the picture was completely developed.

Jackson had to perform the following steps every time he wanted to "make" a wet-plate photograph:

William H. Jackson mixing photographic chemicals while perched atop a mountain.

1. First, he'd coat a glass plate with collodion, a strong-smelling substance that became tacky when it dried. Once sticky, the plate was dunked in a bath of silver nitrate. After two or three minutes, the chemicals would glom together, producing a plate that was sensitive to light.
2. To keep the light out, the photographer would then clamp the glass plate inside a holder. He'd dash over to his camera, insert the plate, and position the lens where he wanted it.

3. Finally, he'd remove the lens cap to expose the picture. Even this last step was tedious since the photographer had to wait for three to six seconds for the picture to fully expose.

A stereoscopic image of White Mountain, or Mammoth Hot Springs, by William H. Jackson.

Summing up the challenges of early photography, Jackson later wrote: "You prayed every time the lens was uncapped."[95]

Another burden for the photographer was handling the large heavy glass plates. Photo enlargements didn't exist yet in 1871, so the size of the glass used dictated the exact size of the picture.

Jackson mostly handled ten- or twelve-inch-long glass plates on expeditions. The West's oversized scenery demanded at least this size, so Jackson loaded Hypo with as many plates as the mule would tolerate.

Jackson also took pictures designed especially for stereoscopes. These binocular-like viewers—similar to today's View-Masters—were a popular form of entertainment in the nineteenth century. When a person looked through the viewers, he or she would see a vivid three-dimensional image. But actually, the user was looking at two images, nearly identical in appearance and perched side by side at the end of the viewer. The technology exploits a marvel of human eyesight; specifically, how the left and right eyes work together to focus on a single object.

Through stereoscopes, middle-class families could enjoy a "virtual" journey to strange and distant lands. And by the 1870s, such lands included the vast scenery of the frontier West, a place most Americans would otherwise never get to see.

Jackson with his mule and supplies.

Like Moran, Jackson knew early in life that he loved art. As a young boy growing up in New York, he drew or painted every day. At fifteen, he got a job in a local studio tinting photographs by hand, a common practice before color photography was invented. Jackson never attended high school or college and so was completely self-taught, finding time—even as a

A young William H. Jackson.

Union soldier during the Civil War—to sketch soldiers and camp life.

But then, a nasty breakup with his fiancée sent him reeling. Years later he couldn't recall exactly what the two had fought over, but Jackson blamed himself. "If I had possessed the wit of a squirrel," he later wrote, "I would have acknowledged my fault . . . and been forgiven."[96] Instead, the flustered twenty-three-year-old headed west, carrying a picture of his sweetheart Caddie, which remained with him the rest of his life.

As Jackson boarded a train headed west—even pawning his watch to cover the cost of a rail ticket—he could see that he wasn't alone. "When times were hard in the East . . . when you left the army after serving through a war, and were restless and footloose—when you had a broken heart, or too much ambition for your own good—there was always the West."[97]

Resourceful and scrappy, Jackson adapted quickly to his new environment. He took a job as a bullwhacker, snapping herds of oxen into action as they pulled

As a bullwhacker, Jackson helped tame half-wild Texas longhorn bulls.

covered wagons across the plains. On one of these journeys, his moccasins were so worn that his feet became badly bruised and numb.

He made pictures whenever he could, desperate for money. He even snapped portraits of ladies who worked in brothels. Finally, he landed a job with the railroads and was able to spend most of his time outdoors again, taking pictures of the windswept plains, mountains, and American Indian tribes, who fascinated him.

One of his best discoveries was finding out, as he later wrote in his autobiography, that "it was possible to do the thing I most wanted to do and get paid for it as well."[98]

Then came the opportunity that changed Jackson's life forever. In July 1870, on his way to survey the Wyoming Territory, Ferdinand Hayden dropped into Jackson's Omaha, Nebraska, studio. Hayden, always on the lookout for new western images, asked to see the photographer's portfolio. While flipping through, he realized he needed Jackson to help him document the West.

Would there be a salary? Jackson wondered, after Hayden offered him a position on his next survey. Hayden smiled and shook his head. The only thing he could offer was "a summer of hard work, and the satisfaction I think you would find in contributing your art to science."[99] Jackson considered the offer, conferring briefly with his wife Mollie, a woman he had come to love who often managed the studio for him while he traveled to take photos. Hayden could offer no compensation to Jackson, but the expedition planner was still taking a financial risk. Photography, with its numerous glass plates and expensive chemicals, was

Glacier Point Rock, 3201 feet.   Yosemite Valley, Cal.   Photo., San Francisco.

Jackson scrambled low—and high—to capture his images.

costly in the nineteenth century. Jackson's supplies alone would eat up one-tenth of Hayden's budget.

Hayden's 1871 expedition would be the first time a camera was carried—or more accurately, saddled, hauled, and wheeled—through Yellowstone. Jackson's massive haul included two cameras, a tripod, a portable dark box, bottles full of chemicals, and hundreds of glass plates—some as large as twenty-by-twenty-four inches.

And now, Jackson stood staring into Tower Falls' deep gorge, wondering how he would ever capture a picture of the entire falls. Ever improvising, Jackson's sturdy figure started to clamber down the rocky slope. The only solution as he saw it: to get to the bottom of the waterfalls as quickly as he could.

Unable to carry the bulky darkroom any further, he left it at the top of the falls. Jackson set up his tripod and camera two hundred feet below, at the base of the falls. For the next few hours he scrambled madly between the two points, shuttling glass plates to and from the falls.

Photographer William H. Jackson triumphed again: one of his hard-won pictures of Tower Falls.

Ever practical, Jackson made use of local resources. To keep the plates from drying out, he and Moran gently wrapped them in cloths moistened in Tower Creek's waters. Finally, after five grueling cycles, Jackson believed he'd captured Tower Falls' essential beauty. For one photograph, he asked Moran to crouch atop a boulder at the bottom of the falls. In the final picture, one can barely see the speck that is Moran. The falls dwarf him completely.

Jackson would still have to worry about the fragile plates surviving the bumpy mule ride through Yellowstone and the train ride back East. But, for now, he'd managed to overcome another hurdle and to capture another of Yellowstone's wonders.

★★★

The next morning Hayden, Peale, and artist Henry Elliott set out to fine-tune their expedition map. In this vast wilderness, only the most basic geography had

been plotted on paper. To fill in the details of the few maps they had, the trio needed the vantage point of a high mountain. So they set off to climb nearby Mount Washburn, one of Yellowstone's tallest peaks. The mountain was named for General Washburn, leader of the previous year's expedition.

A well-worn path led the three men to the top, an indication that indigenous peoples, too, had discovered the usefulness of this summit. Along the way, the trio passed several herds of antelope grazing on the mountain's fresh grasses. Broken shards of rock clattered under their heavy boots. Hayden, astounded by their "exquisite beauty," spied seams of emerald-green malachite running through rock, as well as agates with caramel-colored looping.[100]

Tower Falls today.

Wildflowers on Mount Washburn.

Even more astonishing was the immense panoramic view as they climbed. At ten thousand feet in the air, Hayden, Peale, and Elliott could see for hundreds of miles. In almost every direction, mountains loomed, practically encircling them. Out ahead, the metallic-blue Yellowstone Lake lay shaped like a hand.

The winds "blew terrifically," Peale later wrote.[101] The men had to lie flat on their stomachs to write, otherwise papers would have flown away. Peale helped hold down Elliott's drawing paper, while he hurriedly sketched the surrounding peaks and valleys. Hayden looked around, studying the scenery. The assortment of lines, contours, and jagged peaks spoke volumes about the Earth's history—how its crust had, at various times, buckled, heaved, crumbled, and blew apart.

As Hayden scanned the horizon from this perch in the sky, it soon became clear just what he was looking at. The immense bowl of land that spread before him, encircled by a ring of mountains, was a giant crater. The whole expedition had, in fact, been hiking across an ancient volcano. Its more fiery features would reveal themselves soon enough.

CHAPTER 7
LUDICROUS DESCENT

Were one to fall in, he could be dashed to pieces among the rocks at the bottom.[102]
—Albert Peale, describing Yellowstone's Grand Canyon

The next morning, Peale and Elliott rode their horses to the edge of one of Yellowstone's most stunning vistas—its largest canyon and waterfalls. Standing on its rim, the two men gaped at the huge gouge in the earth. Crashing water thundered over its cliffs.

The pair gazed at the canyon's pink and yellow walls, and, far below, at the thin, green thread of the Yellowstone River. Only moments earlier, they had walked alongside the sprawling river. Now it hurtled itself wildly into the gorge.

The canyon was deep and dizzying. A "second edition of the bottomless pit," wrote an earlier visitor.[103] Many members of the Langford-Washburn party saw it last summer, including Cornelius Hedges. "The view at first is almost terrifying," he wrote, "and makes one's knees knock together."[104]

Even still, the soft-spoken attorney from Massachusetts couldn't help but crawl on his belly and peer over the edge. He did the same thing at other overlooks. "I stayed for hours on these points, almost an entire day," he added. By then "the grand picture" of the canyon had been etched upon his brain, he said—a scene he would recall again and again.[105]

Yellowstone's Grand Canyon.

So many questions came to mind while Peale and Elliott looked at the canyon. How long had it taken the river to carve these giant walls? Where did its colors—startling shades of yellow and pink—come from? Only years of additional science would answer those questions, but there was one that the two young men were willing to tackle: how tall was its falls?

Henry Elliott, Hayden Expedition artist.

A River's Many Moods

The Yellowstone River thunders over cliffs and carves canyons. It also winds lazily through the region's sprawling green valleys—a tranquil watering hole for elk, bison, moose, and numerous other animals.

The more than 600-mile-long river—the largest undammed river in the lower forty-eight states—plays a major role in the geology and ecology of Yellowstone. Its powerful erosive forces sculpted Yellowstone's largest canyon. And as the river climbs and dips over the abruptly changing landscape, it makes two vertical dives, resulting in two of Yellowstone's major waterfalls: the Upper and Lower Falls.

Brink of the Lower Falls.

The Yellowstone River is also the lifeblood of the region. Its surging waters feed the Yellowstone Lake, the largest high-altitude lake (at more than seven thousand feet) in North America. The immense lake provides critical habitat to several species of native fish, including the cutthroat trout, a vital food source of bald eagles and grizzly bears.

The Yellowstone River's cold, rippling waters support numerous bird species. Pelicans, ducks, and geese bob on its surface. Tall and spindly sandhill cranes, with their six-and-a-half-foot wingspans, nest near its banks. The trumpeter swan, snow-white except for its jet-black beak, legs, and feet, is also dependent on the Yellowstone River. The elegant bird—once hunted mercilessly for its eggs, skin, and feathers—is still rarely seen in Yellowstone. But by keeping the Yellowstone River wild and undammed, land managers give imperiled species, like the swan, a fighting chance.

Yellowstone River.   Trumpeter swans.

They knew it would be grueling to climb down the canyon. One of their companions, Robert Adams, Jr., thought it was "ludicrous."[106] Even the local mountain men said it couldn't be done.

Last summer, the Langford-Washburn Expedition estimated the height of the falls by dropping hundreds of feet of marked rope into the canyon. Peale and Elliott hoped to get more precise figures by using a barometer. Hayden needed the data for the report he was preparing for Congress and the country. So the two men made their minds up: they would climb to the bottom of Yellowstone's immense canyon.

It was still morning by the time Peale and Elliott started their descent. The colors on the canyon's walls shifted with the light. They gripped onto pieces of rock as they lowered themselves carefully down, one step at a time. Many of the rocks were crumbly, a result of Yellowstone's inner furnace. Invisible hot vents cook the cliff walls, softening them. The heat also triggers color changes, a chemical reaction similar to the way rain turns exposed metal orange.

With clenched muscles, the men continued on. Now, only about two hundred feet from the bottom, they could see the river's waves chop and hear the falls roar.

Then, just as Peale was lowering his boot for the next step, he realized that there was no place for it to go. He jerked around to look behind him. There was nothing, only air.

Peale and Elliott were clinging to the tip of a jutting nose of rock, a cliff that abruptly ended. Their only choice was to retrace their steps and find a more gradual path down.

They clambered down again, this time moving more swiftly. Their boots kicked up rocks and pebbles. The disruption startled a few hawks nesting nearby. Suddenly, Peale lost his footing. Gripped with fear, he began

The canyon's hard-to-describe colors.

sliding helplessly down the rock face—then stopped. His boots had slammed into solid rock.

The climbers continued scrambling and about an hour later finally reached the bottom of the canyon. The falls pounded so loudly that it was hard to think. Even though it was afternoon, with the sun shining overhead, it was dim at the bottom of the deep crevice. Gazing up, Peale and Elliott could even make out a few faint stars. Peale also noticed how the trees back up on the rim of the canyon appeared to be no bigger than blades of grass.

As Peale teetered on the edges of the river bank, he noticed small steaming pools, colored red, navy blue, and black. He collected a few samples of their stinking contents with glass bottles. He hammered away at various rocks, stuffing as many as he could into his pockets.

Since the climb up would take longer, they didn't have much time to linger on the canyon floor. Quickly, Elliott sketched his surroundings. Both men were relieved that the fragile pocket barometer had survived the hazardous journey down. They would use the round glass tool to calculate the depth of the canyon and the height of the falls. Because a barometer measures the weight of air bearing down on it, the higher a person is in elevation, the "lighter" the air will be. Conversely,

Aneroid barometer.

the lower one is in elevation (especially, say, at sea level), the "heavier" the air will be. So by calculating the difference between the air pressure at the bottom of the canyon and the pressure back on top, Peale and Elliott could determine the difference in elevation between the two points, or, in other words, the depth of the canyon. This they determined to be one thousand feet and the height of the falls at four hundred feet.

How satisfied the pair of hikers must have felt as they started their climb back up. Peale carried as many rock and mineral specimens as he could, stuffing them into pockets, even clenching some in his fists while he climbed up to the canyon's rim. He was certain these hard-won beauties would delight Hayden.

A Risky Hike with Ropes and Pins

The temptation to climb inside Yellowstone's big canyon didn't end with Albert Peale and Henry Elliott. Starting in the 1890s, a businessman with a love of heights escorted visitors on a primitive hike down into the wondrous canyon. The man, H. F. Richardson, known better as "Uncle Tom," blazed a trail into the canyon, consisting of a series of steps, ropes, and rope ladders that extended over

Postcard of stagecoach carrying early tourists to Yellowstone's Grand Canyon.

the craggy cliffs down to the Yellowstone River at the canyon's bottom.

The hike wasn't for the faint of heart. Visitors, including well-to-do city dwellers accustomed only to casual strolls in the local park, would grip fiercely onto the ropes that draped over the sheer walls. Ladies, wearing fashionably long skirts, were offered pins to tie up their dresses to make the climb easier.

Today, a metal staircase consisting of 328 steps takes visitors about halfway down the canyon. Because the second part of the staircase was damaged by heavy snows, visitors can no longer make the dizzying trek to the bottom, as Peale and Elliott did more than 140 years ago.

The climb, however, proved too tedious, and Peale had already had that close call coming down. At one point, he got too nervous. Fearful that he'd "slide to the bottom and be dashed to pieces," Peale opened his grip on some of the rocks and let them roll back in the canyon.[107] Some discoveries would have to wait.

After two hours of climbing, the pair returned to the top. Despite the samples he'd let go, Peale still had several others taken from the steaming belly of Yellowstone's Grand Canyon.

Thomas Moran and William Jackson faced their own obstacles at Yellowstone's great canyon. Moran wished to paint the canyon in its entirety. To see its many viewpoints, he had to crawl out to various ledges—his fingers trembling as he sketched. He stared at the scene, trying to embed the incredible imagery in his brain. Moran relied heavily on his memory to recall scenes when he was back home in his studio. But the canyon's complex colors—from pale yellows to blazing brick red—vexed Moran. How would he ever be able to duplicate them? Some were so faint; others such a bizarre blend.

Field sketch of Yellowstone's canyon by Thomas Moran. Notice his initial sketches done with pencil.

In his doubt, Moran supposedly told Hayden that the canyon's colors were "beyond the reach of human art."[108] He also realized that he didn't have time to draw detailed pictures of the sights he was studying. Instead, he sketched loose impressions. He drew what he felt. Duplications, or "literal transcriptions," as Moran called them, did not count as art, he once wrote.[109]

Moran and Jackson spent the next four days exploring the canyon, remaining there even after the rest of the party had moved on. "Moran's enthusiasm," Jackson noted, "was greater here than anywhere else."[110] During their downtime, the companions shared personal details. They talked about art, the startling

Another rendering of Yellowstone's colorful canyon by Thomas Moran.

imagery of the West, and, undoubtedly, their wives, who both happened to be named Mollie. Jackson's Mollie was expecting their first child. Moran and his wife already had three children.

For now, though, Moran remained transfixed on the massive gorge before him. He lingered at a spot now known as Artist's Point. He must have wondered: Could he do these glowing walls justice? Despite his apprehensions, Moran would go on and try. It would prove to be the largest—and riskiest—undertaking of his career.

CHAPTER 8
WONDERLAND

My fairy books could not equal such wonderful tales. Fountains of boiling water, crystal clear, thrown hundreds of feet in the air . . .[111]

—Emma Cowan, a tourist visiting Yellowstone in 1877

Thanks to Peale's regular reports printed in papers like the *Philadelphia Press*, bits of Yellowstone's magic and mystery began wafting back east. "There is the greatest interest everywhere in the success of our expedition," Hayden happily informed Spencer Baird back at the Smithsonian.[112]

Americans stretched their imaginations as they tried to visualize Peale's colorful descriptions. What must they have thought of his "frozen cascade," or of the hulking slab of rock that signified a "terrible convulsion of nature"?[113] In only two more months, Jackson's snapshots and Moran's lush watercolors would complete the picture for eager and curious readers throughout the country.

Even the skeptics had a hard time hiding their enthusiasm. A "child's fairy tale" was how the *New York Times* described an earlier account of the region. The paper wasn't quite ready to accept Yellowstone as a reality until Hayden's expedition returned with its final report.[114]

With interest in the area growing, a new name for the dazzling place emerged: Wonderland. It was inspired by Lewis Carroll's *Alice's Adventures in Wonderland*, published only years earlier in 1865. After all, Yellowstone's turquoise pools, mud puffs, and jetting geysers seemed to belong to the same world of nonsense inhabited by a shrinking girl, a talking rabbit, and a queen who played croquet with hedgehogs and flamingos.

The nation was slowly forming an attachment to Yellowstone, something that seemed impossible only a decade before.

Yellowstone's steaming terraces, by William H. Jackson.

***

It took centuries, really, before Americans warmed up to nature and the outdoors. In fact, the earliest European settlers despised it. When William Bradford stepped off the *Mayflower* in 1620, he was revolted by the "hideous and desolate wilderness" he discovered.[115] He saw thick, dark tangles of woods that whirred with birds and insects. With ax and ox, settlers hacked away at these primeval forests to make way for crops and sunlit villages.

The early settlers' initial reactions weren't that surprising. Those first Americans were simply echoing the beliefs of their native England, where soft, rolling meadows and farms were the preferred scenery. Mountains and peaks, ugly "bumps" on the horizon, were described as warts, pimples, and blisters, and, in the case of one craggy peak, "Devil's Arse."[116]

American settlers also had trouble connecting with nature because of their fears: in the seventeenth and eighteenth centuries, many New

Northern Pacific Railroad guide.

Daniel Boone guiding settlers through the wilderness. Notice how the settlers are bathed in bright light, while the woods behind them are cast as dark and foreboding.

England Puritans believed that dark forests harbored sinister spirits. "Dragons," "droves of devils," and "fiery flying serpents" lurked there, warned minister Cotton Mather in 1707.[117] The religious zealot, an instigator of the Salem Witch Trials, also linked the woods to witches and witchcraft.

Eventually, science ignited a fresh interest in the universe and the skies. Astronomy, chemistry, and physics became popular fields of

Naturalist and fossil collector Ferdinand Hayden with his geologist's hammer.

study. Advances in printing helped bring these topics to the masses and ignited curiosity. Naturalists tromped across wild spaces in the New World, delighted by its staggering diversity. Geologist Ferdinand Hayden eventually followed suit in his explorations across the western territories of the United States.

Then artists began to offer their fresh perspectives on nature to willing audiences. Poets and painters escaped the soot, smoke, and despair of industrial cities like Boston and New York, and fled to the woods for inspiration.

One of the best known Romantic poets was Lord Byron. "There is pleasure in the pathless woods, there is rapture on the lonely shore," he once wrote.[118] Other writers, including Ferdinand Hayden almost three decades later, would continue to use such flowery language to describe the wonders of America's natural landscape.

Another influential writer was Henry David Thoreau, who made a radical suggestion to Americans in the mid-1800s: get out into nature, he urged listeners. There is peace and spiritual nourishment to be found there. "Our lives," he wrote in 1849, "need the relief of [the wilderness] where the pine flourishes and the jay still screams."[119]

***

Gates of the Yosemite, by Albert Bierstadt. Such imagery introduced Americans to the majesty of their country's scenery.

One of the more powerful emotions that linked Americans to places like Yellowstone was pride. For a long time, the nation was belittled for its lack of sophistication. It didn't have

Henry David Thoreau: Speaking "a Word for Nature"

"Get out and hike," Henry David Thoreau might have said had he been born in the twenty-first century. Instead, Thoreau, one of the most important nature enthusiasts in America, was born in 1817. At that time, when he suggested that people take a walk in the woods to relax and recharge, it was considered a radical idea.

Thoreau challenged Americans to think differently about nature. He found solace as well as inspiration outdoors, and thought others might, too. Nature was unpredictable and exciting, a contrast to the dull and tedious work he saw many Americans engaged in, including his own earlier job of making pencils.

Henry David Thoreau.

An author and lecturer, Thoreau wrote a book about one of his boldest experiments in regards to nature: for almost two years, he lived alone in the remote woods, in a rustic cabin he'd built himself. Why? As he later told surprised audiences, it was because he wanted to live "deep and suck out all the marrow of life."[120]

Thoreau's provocative writings on nature—during his time, but especially in our own—have convinced generations of Americans of the importance of wild spaces in our lives.

The view from Thoreau's hut in Concord, Massachusetts.

the ancient masterpieces that Europe had: the Sistine Chapel, the *Mona Lisa*, or the castles, cathedrals, and countless other works of art that were in abundance back in Europe. "Who reads an American book?" asked English clergyman Sydney Smith in 1820, "or goes to an American play? Or looks at an American picture or statue?"[121]

Abigail Adams.

Eventually Americans realized that they possessed "masterpieces" of their own. Their artwork just happened to be found outdoors. One of the first to openly praise her nation's natural beauty was Abigail Adams. While visiting London in 1784, she bragged to a friend: "Do you know that European birds have not half the melody of ours? Nor is their fruit half so sweet, nor their flowers half so fragrant. . . ."[122]

A Proud President . . . and His Moose

One of the staunchest defenders of America's natural beauty was none other than the nation's third president, Thomas Jefferson. The founding father, inventor, and architect was also a naturalist who bred plants and designed gardens at his Monticello home. Jefferson had a deep appreciation for the young republic's sprawling, undisturbed scenery, which contrasted greatly with the man-made structures and landscapes he saw popping up all over Europe.

Thomas Jefferson, by Rembrandt Peale, 1800.

So when the world-renowned French scientist Comte de Buffon stated in a book that the animals in America were scrawnier than the animals in Europe, Jefferson responded sharply and swiftly. After traveling to France to meet Buffon, Jefferson trotted out physical evidence of the New World's regal creatures, including "an uncommonly large panther skin."[123] But when that wasn't enough to convince the Frenchman of America's impressive wildlife, Jefferson began to boast about the country's moose, an animal so large, he exclaimed, that a European reindeer could walk under its belly. Of course, Buffon wanted proof that such an animal existed.[124]

Jefferson hurriedly sent word to his colleagues in New England to find one. An imposing moose was found, but even before it was loaded on a ship bound for France, the stuffed and preserved specimen had already begun to rot and shed hair. Regardless, Jefferson had made his point and Buffon agreed to make revisions to his world-famous *Natural History* book series.

In time, others, too, came to appreciate America's bounty of natural resources—its mountains, forests, rivers, and streams—much of it still in a pristine, untouched state.

Even more, such scenery and formations had taken thousands, if not millions, of years to form. What could be more ancient than that, proclaimed keen observers, such as Horace Greeley, editor of the *New York Tribune*.

In his travels across the American West, Greeley was awed by the country's giant vistas and strange shapes and forms. But perhaps most mind-boggling to him were California's giant three-thousand-year-old sequoias. Greeley pointed out to his readers that these giants existed long before there were cathedrals and castles. The trees were standing, he wrote, when "David danced before the ark, when Solomon laid the foundations of the Temple,

A stereo image of one of California's mammoth trees, which was seventy-three feet in circumference.

when Theseus ruled in Athens, when Aeneas fled from the burning wreck of vanquished Troy . . ."[125]

By the 1870s, Yellowstone had become America's iconic wonder. Thanks to the Hayden Expedition, people were learning about a wondrous region in their country that might not be rivaled anywhere else in the world. A newspaper reporter for the *New York Herald* bragged, "Why should we go to Switzerland to see mountains or to Iceland for geysers?"[126]

But not everyone was enchanted with Yellowstone's beauty for its own sake. Profiteers, like Jay Cooke, wanted to exploit it for their own purposes. As Yellowstone stood to play a big part in his Northern Pacific

Cover of a Northern Pacific Railroad brochure.

railroad, Jay Cooke remained curious about the people's interest in the region out west. "Keep me informed of the public reaction to Yellowstone," he instructed his publicity manager.[127]

America was still wrestling with her feelings about nature when Hayden and his men marched through Yellowstone. The nation was expanding and growing. Natural resources like gold, timber, and coal were adding to the nation's prosperity and making some people rich. But there was also a growing awareness that something valuable might be lost if the country's people continued to plow, ax, and pick their way across the nation's last wild spaces.

CHAPTER 9
INTO THE DRAGON'S MOUTH

The smell of sulphur is strong but not unpleasant to a sinner.[128]
—Mark Twain, nineteenth-century author and commentator

Peale and Elliott wrapped up their canyon work, tucking notes, sketches, and specimens back into the pockets of their saddlebags. Hours of climbing and scrambling up and down cliffs had left them famished. As they followed the river, though, they knew they had an easy food source: trout.

They caught several fish, but upon slicing them open discovered the fish's stomachs were full of long white worms. Infested, the fish were inedible. The two men would have to wait until they got back to camp.

On their way, they traveled across a broad valley whose velvet-green hills sloped out before them. The Yellowstone River flowed through the lush green flats in the looping shape of a serpent. Given its abundance of grass and fresh water, this area, known today as the Hayden Valley, is a magnet for wildlife.

Peale and Elliott likely saw herds of bison as they rode along. Female bison flock together in groups, guarding their spring-born calves. Bulls, whose snorts can be heard hundreds of feet away, will often be alone, wallowing in cool mud to fend off biting flies.

Wolves are known to prowl Yellowstone's Hayden Valley.

The valley also drew deer and elk, as well as moose that browsed on bushy stands of willow. Birds such as ducks, geese, loons, and bright-white trumpeter swans bobbed on the river. Given the wide assortment of prey, gray wolves often hunt in this valley, tucking themselves behind mounds of sagebrush on the lookout for a lone bison calf or other weak straggler for an evening meal.

A Burly Survivor

Bison are the largest animals in North America. Bulls, or male bison, can weigh two thousand pounds and females one thousand pounds. Today, most bison in the United States live on farms or are raised as livestock for meat, but in Yellowstone wild bison roam freely, with no fences or barbed wire to pen them in.

A bull bison wallowing.

Herds of bison, consisting mostly of females and their young, roam across Yellowstone's vast valleys in search of fresh grasses to graze on. Bulls spend much of their lives alone, except during the mating season or during the rut in late summer, when they compete with other males to establish dominance. During these forceful displays of strength, dueling males will grunt loudly, wallow (or roll in the dirt), and charge at one another.

Calves are born in late April and May and within two to three hours can travel with the rest of the herd. These younger members, however, remain under the careful watch of their mothers and other females, as they're still vulnerable to predators such as wolves and grizzly bears. If a female bison senses a calf is in danger, she'll charge fiercely—which

A bison calf.

is why it's never a good idea to approach a bison calf (or any wild animal), as gentle as it might look.

With their thick fatty skin and dense fur and beards, bison are exquisitely adapted to surviving Yellowstone's harsh winters. They also possess unusually large heads that they use like snowplows, pushing aside ice and snow to access the green foliage underneath.

The rugged bison is a powerful symbol of the American spirit. But sadly, this tough creature, which once numbered forty to sixty million animals

in the United States, was almost hunted to extinction. Thankfully, Yellowstone's early custodians shielded the region's last wild animals from gunfire, and because of their foresight, visitors to today's park can still see descendants of the lumbering giants that once roamed the country.

Bison trudging through deep Yellowstone snows.

★★★

While Peale and Elliott were following the Yellowstone River back to meet the rest of the team, Hayden and a small party of men marched on towards the watery hand they had spied atop Mount Washburn: Yellowstone Lake. The lake was a primary destination for Hayden, as it had been for the Langford-Washburn party. More like an inland sea, the mountaintop lake feeds several of the region's rivers and tributaries.

As the party rode on, the landscape shifted. Gone were the thick stands of crisp-smelling pine and the bright cliffs of the canyon. The land that spread before them now appeared barren, dead. The men squinted at its bleached rubble. Numerous pits and craters—ranging in size from tiny pores to holes as wide as swimming pools—scarred its surface. Instead of trees, ghostly smoke figures swirled up from cracks in the earth, hissing and seething as they fought to escape.

One of Yellowstone's steaming landscapes.

Gold hunters who had marched through the area in 1867 called it Hell.[129] A similar scene in Yellowstone reminded European tourist Lord Dunraven of a ravaged city "sunk amid flames into the bowels of the earth."[130]

Hayden treaded through thick, moist vapors that hung on him like a cloak. The sulfurous fumes stunk of spoiled eggs and tarnished his silver watch. He tested the earth's surface, threading his way carefully around dozens of boiling pots and vents. The ground felt hollow and a bit unsteady, but the farther he walked the more assured he became that he "could walk over it anywhere."[131]

Suddenly a deep rumbling sound, like the roar of an incoming train, grabbed his attention. As he walked towards it, the sound reverberated even louder. Its source, however, turned out to be just a small hole in the ground, a miniature chimney about as wide across as Hayden's hand. He called it Locomotive Jet.

All around the steaming vent, the earth was crumbly and deposited in fine layers similar to a pie crust. Hayden used a stick to probe at its flaky surface. Hot steam erupted immediately and revealed clusters of neon-yellow gems. He recognized their source: sulfur! Sulfur was also responsible for the rotten-egg smell.

The men couldn't help but poke at the crust and uncover more of the gaudy crystals. "We took pleasure in breaking it up . . ." Hayden wrote later, "and exposing the wonderful beauty."[132]

Farther on, Hayden spied a large cloud of steam gushing from the earth. He hiked in closer, through

Sulfur crystals near a steam vent.

a curtain of hot fog that temporarily blinded him. Even though he had trouble seeing for several seconds, he heard fiercely bubbling water and smelled more nauseating sulfur fumes. He walked toward the source of the steam but suddenly stopped. The heat was simply too unbearable.

Finally a gust of air broke the curtain of steam and revealed a large seething pool. It was a "magnificent sulphur spring," Hayden later wrote, about fifteen feet across.[133]

Its water was crystal clear. Bubbles raced to the surface. Watching it, Hayden noticed that its simmering grew louder. Larger clouds of steam puffed into the sky.

Unusual formations frame a geyser crater, from a vintage postcard by Frank J. Haynes.

Then, suddenly, the center of the pool surged and began lifting itself up—first one, two, then three and four feet up out of the middle of the pool! Boiling waters flooded the crater and poured out the sides of the rim. Hayden dashed away from the steaming streams. The temperature of the spring, which he eventually called Sulphur Spring, was 197 degrees Fahrenheit.

There was even more to the haunting natural feature. After Sulphur Spring had quieted itself and the steam clouds had dissipated, Hayden explored the unusual rock formations surrounding it. The larger lumps resembled oversized, cooked marshmallows; others were like small bumps and blisters.

There were also unexpected splashes of color, due to the presence of iron, sulfur, and other Earth elements. Streaks of gold, green, and red oozed through

The swirling, stinking contents of a mud pot.

punctured crust of earth. These bizarre sculptures captivated Hayden.

After passing through a small island of trees, Hayden encountered a bleak stretch of earth with more craters. They sloshed with gray, brown, and black fluids. Some were watery and thin, and others thick as pudding, Hayden noted. Their different consistencies produced varying sounds: one wheezed, another groaned, and still another sounded like someone gargling.

Hayden explored the burbling pots. It was obvious that the Earth's crust was softer here, no longer brittle. But he wanted to examine a couple more, and scampered a few steps forward. On the last step, Hayden plunged through the crust and fell up to his knees in scorching mud.

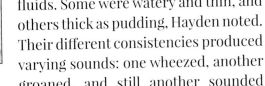

Peale and Elliott returned to camp, ate heartily, then set out again to explore some of the same steaming features that Hayden was investigating. Peale crept

Mountain Medicine

From cuts and bruises to broken bones and burns, injuries were common on western expeditions. Men scraped themselves on jagged rocks and broken tree branches. They tripped over projecting roots and rocks. They slid down cliffs and sometimes fell from high mountain perches as they attempted to orient themselves in a strange land.

The misfortune of falling into Yellowstone's steaming mud, as depicted in Nathaniel Langford's article for *Scribner's Monthly.*

In the hot, soupy thermal basins of Yellowstone, Hayden and his men scalded themselves on boiling springs, some of which were also highly acidic. Their feet sank through undetected patches of scalding mud, which clung to their skin and caused excruciating pain.

Many injuries resulted from handling horses and mules. Mules kicked men when the animals resisted heavy loads and tight cinching. Horses, panicked by the sounds of wild animals, often tossed riders and caused broken bones and head injuries.

Treatment for such wounds was basic. Bandages were usually on hand, as were mild pain relievers, but unusual forms of trauma had to be handled creatively and with a high risk of complications.

Lieutenant Gustavus Doane, while traveling with the 1870 Washburn-Langford Expedition, developed a painful infection in his thumb. For several days he was plagued with throbbing pain that he tried to numb by dunking his hand in icy streams. Finally, when the swelling caused his whole hand to balloon up, and nonstop pain robbed him of several days of sleep, Doane agreed to a crude operation. Using a penknife, fellow party member Nathaniel Langford sliced open Doane's thumb, right through to the bone.

Fortunately, the "surgery" relieved Doane's misery and the infection. After two straight days of sleep, the military man and explorer recovered and was up chronicling Yellowstone's unusual wonders again.

The roiling, stinking Dragon's Mouth Spring, which was documented by Hayden's 1871 expedition.

up to a pool that sloshed with a noxious yellow-green brew. Another was more cavernous. Its waters sloshed against its inner wall, sounding like waves slamming against the shore. It belched foul-smelling steam continuously. Regardless, the inquisitive Peale couldn't help but note: "It would be a delightful place for a vapor bath."[134]

In putting a small sample of water to his mouth he discovered it tasted sour. A later visitor compared a mouthful of hot spring water to a "diabolic julep of Lucifer matches, bad eggs, vinegar, and magnesia."[135]

In the previous year's expedition, such stinking pools had reminded Langford of the witches in William Shakespeare's play, *Macbeth*. As Langford stared into the pools' vile, roiling waters, he couldn't help but envision "the 'black and midnight hags' concocting a charm around this horrible cauldron."[136] Another member of that expedition, Cornelius Hedges, was reminded of other haunting images; when Langford's group visited a spring called Hell-Broth Springs, Hedges's mind filled with images of "grimy ghosts and demons dire."[137]

Up ahead, Peale could see some of the other men in the expedition, including the doctor. Hayden's accident had caused him "great pain," he reported, but the explorer seemed back to his usual self quickly, focused on a massive steaming pit.[138]

The feature was a large pool, about thirty feet across, churning with a gray-brown liquid. The corpses of toppled trees were slung around its crater. The evergreen trees behind them were splattered with dried mud.

Yellowstone's springs may not only boil—some are as acidic as battery acid.

The men were listening to an old trapper who'd crossed this country before. He told them the massive pool would blow just after sundown. That hardly seemed possible: the pool was calm and flat, aside from a column of small bubbles rising from its center. Was this just another exaggerated mountain man story?

A mud feature known today as Red Spouter.

Then the water began to bubble more fiercely. A wave of murky water started to rise. It climbed to three feet, then died away. It rose up again. And again. Then came a rumbling like suffocated thunder along with big puffs of steam. In a flash, brown water blew out of the crater. It shot up twenty feet, with some of the burst going even higher!

The mud gusher thundered on for another twenty minutes, then stopped as suddenly as it began. With so much water expelled, the pool of muddy water had receded significantly. It became "as smooth as the most placid lake," Peale recorded later in his journal.

According to the trapper, to whom the men now listened attentively, the mud gusher erupted a total of four times a day. Wishing for more detailed notes about the phenomenon, Hayden asked one of the assistants to watch the mud crater for the next twenty-four hours.

The others headed back to camp to turn in. They couldn't wait to see, as Peale wrote in his journal, "what wonder this country will produce next."[139]

CHAPTER 10
WAVES

Usually in the morning the surface of the lake is calm, but toward noon and after, the waves commence to roll and the white caps rise . . .[40]

—Ferdinand Hayden

The next morning, the men continued taking more measurements of the sloshing mud features. Hayden returned to the site of his accident, determined to gather more information about the boiling mud pots. This time, of course, he knew where not to step. Peale worked diligently beside him, dipping glass bottles into the vats of steaming goo. Their exact contents would be determined later by scientists at the Smithsonian Institution.

Bleary-eyed, the man posted to the overnight geyser-watch returned and announced that the Mud Gusher had erupted another *two times* overnight. Apparently, the grizzled mountain man was right: the mud crater was a regular performer that appeared to spew its contents every six hours. This provided even more data for Hayden to drop into his rapidly growing report.

By afternoon, the whole party was pushing on towards the lake once again. The men continued to track the Yellowstone River, their constant guide, as it wove through stands of pine- and wildflower-specked meadows. Vivid color had again returned to the landscape. Pretty soon the expedition was within sight of the large, 130-mile-wide Yellowstone Lake.

The lake was an immense body of water with waves that crashed and foamed like the ocean. A curious speck of land rose up from its center: an island carpeted with trees.

The party found an ideal spot for camp, a broad grassy opening sheltered by trees. "Lake view," as they called it, offered an abundant

Men rounding Yellowstone Lake.

Hook It, Then Cook It

It's been called "Fish Pot," "Chowder Pot," and "Fisherman's Kettle." This hot spring, which burbles atop a cone-shaped mound, is located on the shores of Yellowstone Lake. Mountain men, such as Jim Bridger, were among the first to make it famous when they raved how an angler could nab an instant supper by pulling a trout from the lake and plunking it in the adjacent boiling spring.

This natural "kitchen" in the wilds of Yellowstone was likely used by indigenous peoples for centuries, but it was first recorded by a member of the Washburn-Langford party, who discovered it by accident. One of the men had hooked a trout, but when he swung back his pole to pull the fish out, the trout flew off and landed, it just so happened, right in the simmering spring. As another party member later recounted, it didn't take long before the fish was "literally boiled."

Fishing Cone eventually became a popular tourist attraction, and visitors donned kitchen aprons and chef hats as they posed for pictures with it. Eventually, heavy traffic around the cone caused damage to the spring as well as injuries to visitors, including one angler, in 1921, who suffered extensive burns when the cone spontaneously erupted. For these reasons, it's illegal for today's visitors to Yellowstone to stand on Fishing Cone, although it can be easily viewed from a nearby trail.

Vintage postcard by Frank J. Haynes.

supply of fresh mountain water for drinking and bathing, plenty of grass for the animals, and more trout than the men could catch in a lifetime.

Exploring the lake and its hundreds of miles of shoreline was one of Hayden's group's most ambitious undertakings, so the men were immediately directed to get to work on building a boat. Mules had already hauled the clunky twelve-foot

The Hayden Expedition's camp at Yellowstone Lake, by William H. Jackson.

wooden frame across hundreds of miles of valleys, streams, and canyons. All that remained was the final assembly of the various pieces. The men wrapped the frame tightly with a sturdy canvas and waterproofed it with tar. They carved oars out of nearby pine trees and repurposed the only suitable material they had for a sail: a woolen horse blanket.

They named the little vessel *Annie*, but the attribute is not entirely clear. The name may have been inspired by one of the young men's girlfriends. But Anna was also the name of the daughter of the influential Congressman Henry L. Dawes, who helped champion the congressional money needed for the expedition.

The boat *Annie*.

Amid cheers, the men launched the boat out into Yellowstone Lake. Peale soon reported that it "rides quite well."[141] But there must have been doubts: could the "little boat," as Hayden called it, survive the lake's powerful six-foot-waves? The boat sent out last year by

Langford and his party shattered after only one hour. Hypothermia was a grave danger as the lake waters averaged only between forty and fifty degrees Fahrenheit in the summer.

The first real test of the boat's integrity came the next morning when James Stevenson, Hayden's chief assistant, and Henry Elliott set their sights on Yellowstone Lake's largest island. The trip was four miles each way and took most of the day, but the two men returned safely by late afternoon. They recounted their adventures and told about the thick vegetation on the island that reminded them of a jungle, and how they spied numerous animal tracks, including many made by wolves. Hayden eventually named the over one-mile-long island Stevenson Island, in honor of his tireless assistant.

In a few days, Elliott would begin the enormous task of sketching the entire perimeter of the lake—every inlet and cove. It was evening now, though, and time to rest.

★★★

Two men set out in the boat again the next morning. John Beaman, who was responsible for recording all weather and astronomical data during the survey, rigged a system for measuring the lake's depth. It was a crude method, roughly the same used by sailors for centuries to guard boats against grounding in deceptively shallow waters. Beaman attached a long line—hundreds of feet of rope—to a small platform he'd built on the back of the boat. Attached to the tip of the rope was a heavy lead weight. Once the group was ready to measure the depth of a certain point on the lake, they would toss out the rope whose heavy lead would help it sink

Underwater Bubblers

If we could somehow tip Yellowstone Lake over and dump out all of its water, we'd discover a world filled with canyons, sizzling springs, and soaring geysers. Using a submersible robot, scientists working in Yellowstone today have sketched out much of the topography of this bizarre underwater landscape.

Not far from Stevenson Island, named in 1871 after Hayden's faithful assistant, the scientists discovered a canyon that plunges 390 feet down—a

Yellowstone Lake is the largest high-elevation lake in the lower forty-eight states.

figure that would have likely surprised Hayden, who many years earlier declared the lake to be no deeper than 300 feet. The researchers have also discovered large tubes of glasslike silica rising up from the lake floor.

Given the presence of such thermal features, temperatures vary widely beneath the lake—with one spot measuring 252 degrees Fahrenheit! And the top layer of water, which ranges from 40 to 60 degrees Fahrenheit during the summer months, can cause hypothermia, and even death, if swimmers linger in the chilly waters for more than twenty minutes.

Because of its diverse temperatures, Yellowstone Lake nurtures a range of life—from heat-loving algae and microbes, to several native trout species that require cold temperatures for survival.

Avocets over Yellowstone Lake.

to the bottom. Then, they counted how many feet of rope were dropped beneath the water.

Meanwhile, Hayden gathered a small party to embark on the next mission: to investigate Yellowstone's famed geyser basin, where the region's largest and showiest fountains reportedly gushed. Along for the trip would be two of his most hard-working assistants: Peale, to measure and describe the geological wonders, and Elliott, to sketch them.

To map the region, Hayden also needed his topographer, Anton Schonborn, as well as a person to guide the clunky horse-and-cart-drawn odometer. The odometer, attached to a wheel on the cart, tracked distance based on how many times the wheel rotated. It was a cumbersome system, but the best one available at the time for measuring distance in the field.

Horse with odometer.

Rounding out the group was a cook, an animal packer, and their guide, Jose, who had traveled through the area before. The rest of the men would remain at camp by the lake to continue exploring the massive body of water and its surrounding landscape.

Hayden's party had now been in Yellowstone for two weeks and, given the brief summer season, had only a few more weeks left to explore the geyser basins *and* to complete their detailed journey around the lake. Heavy snows prematurely ended last summer's expedition, a scenario Hayden wished to avoid if at all possible. He decided to allot six days to exploring the geyser basin. That would leave enough time to march north, adjacent to the lake, before heading home.

With an experienced Yellowstone traveler as a guide and a top-notch crew, Hayden was confident they would not have any trouble completing the task in time.

CHAPTER 11
GUSH!

We found ourselves once more in the dominions of the Fire King.[142]
—Lieutenant Gustavus Doane, a member of the 1870 Langford-Washburn party

Hayden's small party bound for the land of bubbling fountains departed on the morning of July 31. The excitement must have been palpable as they contemplated upcoming wonders that Langford had described as "entirely out of the range of human experience."[143]

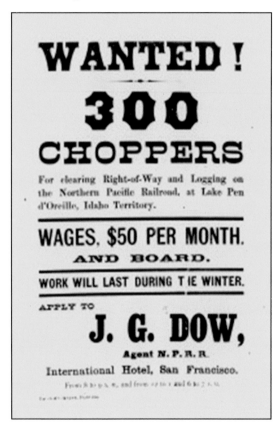

WANTED !

300

CHOPPERS

For clearing Right-of-Way and Logging on the Northern Pacific Railroad, at Lake Pen d'Oreille, Idaho Territory.

WAGES, $50 PER MONTH.
AND BOARD.

WORK WILL LAST DURING TIE WINTER.

APPLY TO

J. G. DOW,

Agent N. P. R. R.

International Hotel, San Francisco.

The Northern Pacific railroad recruited young men to help log forests and clear the way for new railroads.

But reports of fresh dangers threatened to dampen the anticipatory buzz. The previous day, a man rushed into camp with alarming news. There had been an attack in Fort Ellis. American Indians had killed three men and chased off three hundred cattle and horses.

The news of the uprising spread quickly. Within five days, papers back on the East Coast had reported the incident. And one of them, the *Philadelphia Inquirer,* added this grim prognosis: "Further trouble is expected."[144]

The American Indians, it turned out, were Sioux, who were still angry over Northern Pacific railroad crews roving on their ancestral lands. These crews were scouting out the easiest route on which to build Jay Cooke's western-bound railroad. If it meant trespassing on tribal lands, so be it, insisted Cooke.

Cooke had continued to follow the public's growing fanfare surrounding Wonderland—especially Hayden's expedition. If the rumors were correct, and such spectacular scenery existed, he planned on driving the Northern Pacific's tracks as close to Yellowstone as possible.

Meanwhile, Hayden and his men were still moving forward. Given their ambitious agenda—six days to find and document the region's most stunning geysers and then return to the main camp—the men had little time to think about the recent bloodshed. So, with a pink-orange sun rising at their backs, the party struck west for Yellowstone's famed geyser country.

The Firehole is the valley encompassing most of the region's geysers. It's also the name of the river, an offshoot of the Madison, which courses through Yellowstone's western boiling landscape. It's this river that inspired one of mountain man Jim Bridger's cleverest yarns: according to Old Gabe, the river waters racing feverishly over its rocky bottom were the source of friction.

For most of the morning, the party traveled across familiar scenery. From the tops of hills and ridges, they gazed out on the soft green sprawl of the Hayden Valley, where thousands of bison, mere brown specks in the distance, grazed. They passed bone-colored hills where Sulphur Spring and its clan of fuming neighbors hissed and spit.

Hayden and his men rode through thick woods that quickly grew dark. Perfectly straight trees grew out of the forest bed as densely as the hairs on a dog; "Dog-hair stands," observers would later call Yellowstone's choked pine forests. Though silent, the trees were caught in a vicious struggle, each one battling to seize a larger scrap of the bright sunlit canopy high above.

Many, however, had already perished in the struggle. The men's horses stepped easily over fallen trees. The haphazard piles of dead trees, strewn like giant Pick-Up Sticks, were a different story. Fire and wind had caused charred chaos. Lightning strikes trigger fires that sweep through the crowded stands and burn up the weakest members. Gusts of wind, as powerful as gales in a tropical storm, then slam the scorched trees to the ground.

It was sheer misery trying to find a passageway through the thicket of

View through canopy of crowded lodgepole pines.

Fiery Birth

Wildfire has always been a part of the greater Yellowstone ecosystem. Natural fires clear the dead, weakened members in forests and open up space for new plant species. In turn, diversified plant communities support more types of animals, birds, and insects. And while fire-scorched trees may look dreary and desolate, the black snags provide important habitat for cavity-nesting birds, such as bluebirds, which seek out hollow trunks for nesting.

Bluebird near cavity of dead tree.

Given the frequency of fire in the region, Yellowstone's trees have evolved numerous strategies for coping with intense heat and flames. One tree, the Douglas fir, has even adapted to explosive lightning strikes, which can rip strips of bark from trees and hurl them hundreds of feet away. The tree does this by accumulating an extra-thick outer bark that shields its more vulnerable water-delivering tissues from heat.

Wildland fire.

Other trees dodge fire by growing higher in the mountains, where temperatures are cooler and less conducive to fires. At higher altitudes, forests are also sparser and thinner, so less fuel material is available to feed a potential fire.

But no tree is better adapted for wildfires than the lodgepole pine. This evergreen tree may look lanky, but evolution has endowed it with a most clever form of fire insurance. The lodgepole produces two kinds of pinecones, each of which houses a specific kind of seed. One type of pinecone germinates under normal, non-fire conditions. The other, specially designed for blazing heat, is sealed up in a hard sticky resin. Temperatures must reach 113 degrees Fahrenheit before this type of pinecone's hard resin melts and its precious seeds are released. This ensures that even in the case of a wildfire, lodgepole seeds will continue to spread and germinate.

downed logs. The cart that carried the odometer got repeatedly jammed between trees and required painstaking extrication. The men cursed as tree branches scratched their faces and as jutting logs battered their legs. Resistant mules and horses added to the overall frustration. The men cracked whips to spur on the animals and were forced to yank along especially stubborn animals on foot.

The tangle of trees extended for miles and "threatened to obstruct our passage altogether," Hayden later recalled.[145] Yet the indomitable crew soldiered on. They spied a clearing up ahead, a mirage that coaxed them forward. Freshly inspired, they picked up their pace. But after logging only a couple miles, they found themselves facing another maddening roadblock of fallen trees.

The scenario replayed again and again for a total of thirty-one miles. Finally, completely exhausted, the men broke for camp. It was past sundown now, and the whole bunch was ravenous. They hurried through essential camp chores, eager to eat supper, which consisted of coffee, bread, and elk meat.

Then, everyone besides the unfortunate chap assigned guard duty collapsed for the night, huddled beneath woolen blankets and the glittering spray of stars.

***

August 1. It was obvious, again, that the group was traveling inside a sleeping volcano. The men spied fingers of smoke wafting above trees and craters that pocked the ground. They passed a stream lined in white, a substance Hayden recognized immediately: it was sinter, or geyser rock, a hard volcanic rock that forms the basis of many of the region's underground conduits. It constitutes the sturdy piping in Yellowstone's vast plumbing network, which is capable of zipping the scalding two-hundred-degree waters to numerous points underground.

The white milky deposits in this basin are due to siliceous sinter, or geyserite.

The men spied pots of boiling mud, similar to the ones at Sulphur Spring. In this strange land, two craters could bubble alongside each other and look entirely different—one crystal-clear, hot and gently simmering; the other a burbling gray-brown pot with contents as thick as oatmeal.

Despite all that bubbled and brewed around them, there was little to eat that night. Jose had no meat to offer them. He'd shot at a buffalo, but the large bull stormed off before the hunter could fire any more shots.

Telltale curling chimneys of steam give away the location of nearby hot springs and geysers.

★★★

August 2. It had been a cold, uncomfortable night. The men woke up that morning to find sheets of ice under their blankets. Their stomachs felt hollow due to last night's sparse dinner.

Feeling stiff and sore, the group grabbed cups of thin black coffee and gazed out on the smoking valley in front of them. Hayden compared the scene to a factory village, with its hundreds of smoke columns flooding the sky with steam. In the chilly air, vents that were once invisible could now be easily spotted. The freezing temperatures acted like ultraviolet light at a crime scene, exposing many curious specimens that otherwise would have escaped notice.

Hayden and Peale hiked to the basin they had noticed in the distance the day before. Padding across warm crusty earth, they came to a large stretch of steaming pink mush. It was enclosed in a crater about the width of a large house. Inside the crusty rimmed crater, bubbles of fine white mud spluttered and plopped. "Mud Puffs," Hayden called the quirky leaping bits of mud. "The surface is covered with twenty or thirty of these puffs," he noted, "which are bursting every second."[146]

Over time, the little ejections of mud formed

A "mud puff," or paint pot.

small delicate cones, rings, and circles. The mud varied in color, too, Hayden noted, from "the purest white to bright, rich pink."[147] Peale bottled up small samples of the steaming clay, which measured 140 degrees Fahrenheit.

They found other springs, including one with "a beautifully scalloped rim" that made a dull rocking sound.[148] Hayden called it Thumping Geyser.

By the time they returned to camp, Hayden, Peale, and the other men learned that Jose had not found food, *again*. Hayden and his survey manager, Stevenson, had expected meat from hunting excursions to supply the bulk of the men's daily calories. The small quantities of dry goods they'd carried with them—coffee and flour for biscuits and pancakes—would not be enough to sustain eight men for the four days they had left in the geyser basin.

The remaining flour supply would now have to be strictly rationed. And until meat came in, their only other choice was to hunt down birds and small animals. Whether or not the men succeeded in capturing food that evening is unknown. No man writes of eating dinner in his journal.

✶

TOSSING THE FLAPJACK.

Sketch of camp life on a western expedition.

August 3. Each man eagerly prepared his own breakfast the next morning. When it was Peale's turn, he mixed together water and a bit of rationed flour—then poured cupfuls of the thin batter onto a sizzling pan. Flapjacks. They were small and bland, but to the ravenous Peale, they tasted "quite good."[149]

As Hayden had already gone out to explore the nearby hills, Peale stayed back to pack specimens, including those gathered at the Mud Puffs.

Meanwhile, Hayden was exploring a stretch of white crumbly earth. He noticed the remains of trees, slender bright-white corpses that poked straight out of the ground. Others had collapsed and were lying flat or had fallen into the steaming waters.

In this ever-changing landscape, boiling waters can erupt suddenly at the ground's surface and flood existing trees and plants. The tree roots, accustomed to slurping up whatever solution is around them, soak up the hot silica-rich waters and deliver them to thirsty trunks and limbs. Over time, the unfortunate trees slowly turn themselves into a sort of glass.

"Ghost" trees, victims of Yellowstone's hot, silica-rich waters.

It's hard not to find stark beauty in their death, though. Hayden found many specimens of these silicified remains. There were pinecones caked in the white glaze. And later, Peale found a butterfly embalmed with the white substance. The insect had obviously made the fatal mistake of confusing a blazing hot pool with one full of fresh water.

As Hayden trudged on, he became acutely aware of his thirst. The men were accustomed to refilling their canteens throughout the day with ice-cold lake or stream water. It had been hours now since Hayden had filled his. Frustrated, he continued walking past pools of crystal clear water. Many had flooded their craters and formed streaming channels that oozed far away from their blue-hot source. These run-off channels were saturated with color: creamy orange, and the yellow of scrambled eggs. In some, fine green fibers vibrated in the gentle flow of the waters.

The sound of trickling water must have tortured the thirsty Hayden. It had been eight hours now since he'd had something to drink. He gazed

Hayden passed by many hot springs, but none were suitable to drink.

out to the base of the closest mountain a few miles away. It would be his best chance for finding fresh water. During summer, hills at the base of mountains collect the melting snows that drain from the higher white-capped peaks.

Hayden rode his horse out to the hill and began climbing its nearly vertical face. He hunted around for signs of fresh water: a patch of green, a moist spot . . . and then, finally, he discovered a small spring "so imbedded in its bright green carpet of moss that it could hardly be seen."[150] Hayden pulled out the invading clumps of moss and situated his canteen up against the crystal clear waters. He filled his canteen repeatedly.

After hydrating himself, Hayden saw that Peale had joined him. The two planned to explore the basin a little more before heading back to camp. After riding a few miles, they noticed that their horses' hooves were starting to leave thick imprints on the ground.

They were crossing steaming mud, and now their horses were sinking in more deeply. If the animals became frightened, they would likely toss the men out of their saddles. It was a scenario that one of Langford's men had experienced last summer. A man was on his horse when suddenly his animal plunged into mud up to its belly. Panicked from pain and a loss of footing, the animal threw the man over its head. The man landed, hands and elbows first, into the scalding mud.

A variety of heat-tough microorganisms thrive in hot spring waters.

Fortunately, after tedious backtracking and some luck, Hayden and Peale managed to avoid a similar episode. They detoured widely around the steaming sands and headed back to camp. But their good fortune was short-lived. When the pair returned to camp they received the same dismal news they'd gotten the last three nights: Jose, despite scouring the valley all day for game, had been unable to find any meat for the men to eat.

There was one piece of good news, though. Henry Elliott had managed to shoot a duck earlier with his pistol. Better yet, he was willing to share. It would be Hell Fire Stew for dinner. Like the resourceful mountain men in Yellowstone before them, Hayden's men would cook their meat over a simmering hot pot.

★★★

August 4. The next morning, Hayden, Peale, and Schonborn, the topographer, headed out to map and measure more hot springs.

They hiked up to a small cascade they heard rushing over the side of a hill. Compared to the thundering falls in the canyon, this waterfall fell in a long silver cord down the side of the cliff. Several feet down it struck a massive boulder and shattered into many smaller falls. The men walked its base, where moss carpeted the rocks. The name, Fairy Falls—given by an earlier party—seemed fitting.

The party continued on their march along the Firehole River. They passed pools that frothed up suddenly—"spasmodic springs," Hayden called them.[151] They also saw a boiling pot with a strange toadstool-like rim. Nothing, however, caught their eye like the tremendous steam cloud they saw up ahead. Sitting on top of a hill, it glowed in distinct orange, yellow, and blue layers.

The men hurried to see what was blurring the skies. They climbed a hill, cut through a wall of steam, and discovered one of the largest craters they'd ever seen. It looked bright blue, due to the reflection of the sky above. Its water was so transparent that the men could see white bulbous rocks that lined its throat one hundred feet below.

Grand Prismatic Springs.

They walked on, through blinding hot fog that moistened their clothes. Their boots sank into cushiony earth. Under a thin layer of hot water, a slimy substance streaked yellow and orange across the ground; it was the same coloring reflected in the massive steam cloud.

Up ahead, the men gaped at the most tremendous spring they'd come across yet. It stretched as wide as a lake. (Scientists would later pinpoint its width at 370 feet.) Seen from above, the mammoth pool looked like a deep-blue orb with far-reaching orange tentacles. Hayden called it "Great Spring."

The thousands of gallons of water that spilled out of the huge crater rushed down the sides of the hill. It formed numerous small waterfalls that were also stained with the orange goo.

After trekking back after their breathtaking find, the group received bad news once again: there was still no meat. Though Hayden never admitted it in his communications with Spencer Baird at the Smithsonian, the shortage of food had become a serious problem for the expedition.

Food scarcity wasn't uncommon on western expeditions. In fact, on another of Hayden's trips, a few starving men resorted to eating a hedgehog, to which one man quipped, trying to keep his humor intact, "We didn't get hedgehog every day."[152]

Survey teams hardly had room to tote pounds of food into the wilderness. Even if they could, foods like meat and dairy spoil quickly without proper refrigeration. So hunters, typically locals acquainted with a certain area, were hired to track and kill deer, elk, bison, or bear for supplementary meat.

What challenged hunters during expeditions was trying to track the movements of wild animals. Wildlife may suddenly relocate for many reasons: to find food, to dodge extreme heat or cold, or to avoid biting flies and mosquitoes. And something similar had apparently sent the local deer, elk, and bison running. As a result, the men were forced to hunt down squirrels again, stripping the animal of the little meat it provided and going to bed still quite hungry.

Wildlife may migrate for many reasons: heat, biting insects, or to avoid predators.

***

August 5. It hadn't been a restful night of sleep for the weary crew. Shortly after turning in, they were jarred awake by sudden vibrations. The ground they lay upon was shaking. Then, there were loud whooshing sounds, followed by pelting rains.

A geyser! The first major gusher they'd encountered thus far. But they were simply too fatigued to move. They decided to wait until the morning to explore it.

Soon after, freezing temperatures had them trembling again. Peale woke up "shivering with cold."[153] Like most of the men, he had only a couple thin woolen blankets to keep him warm. All he could do was to wrap them around him more tightly and to try to get a few hours' rest.

Hayden Expedition at camp. Hayden is seated with white hat and glasses. Albert Peale is standing on the far right.

Given the cold temperatures that morning, the men woke up to find a valley filled with swirling steam. The group was eager to see the mighty geyser that had jostled them awake in the night, so a few of the men, including Hayden and Peale, set off in search of it.

Peale dunked his thermometer into pools as they marched along. Schonborn charted their locations on maps. The party was entering the most concentrated stretch of geysers and hot springs in the world.

The weary group crossed the rushing waters of the Firehole River, whose white banks were streaked in an orange-Creamsicle color. Scattered across the ground were more pinecones preserved in white crusty silica. Gray spindles, the remains of former trees, stood erect.

Firehole River.

The team studied a cluster of pools, including one that frothed, rumbled, and splattered for several minutes. Once it was done, Hayden crouched down to examine its rim, which was lined with pearl-like sinter beads. Miniature bubbles fizzed around its edges, leading him to call it Soda Geyser.

With a hammer, Hayden started chipping away at one of the opalescent stones when suddenly the pool started grumbling. The dome of water swelled and lifted itself up, then burst into the air. Hayden sprinted away just in time.

There were countless other pools that bubbled and brewed. One spring, measuring five by ten feet, had sinter steps that naturally climbed from the ground to its rim. Bath-Tub Geyser, Hayden named it. Other gurgling springs were contained inside craters and chimneys that rose up from the ground. Not perfectly round or square, the chimneys were crenulated like the waves of fossilized coral or the margins of a leaf.

With little time to waste, Hayden relied on his first impressions when coming up with names for the features. There were springs they called Punchbowl and Dental Cup, and geysers they named Conch, Horn, and Catfish.[154]

What stood out most about the hot springs, though, were their crystal clear waters that reflected the blue spectrum of light in the sky above. "I can compare it to nothing but the blue of a clear sky," wrote Peale, "and even then you must imagine the color intensified."[155]

To Hayden, it seemed as if one could look forever into one of the springs. And during the day, sunlight bounced off the inner rock corridors and formations, revealing what he called "a wild weird beauty."[156]

The men finally arrived at the source of last night's jolting gusher. All was quiet for the moment. They might have expected a sizable crater, like the tall cuff framing nearby Giant geyser. Instead, this geyser's mouth looked more like a medium-sized hot spring—a hot tub only halfway full.

The water in this brilliant hot spring is actually clear. Its waters absorb the colors of sunlight except one—blue—which is reflected back to our eyes.

Peale climbed across the bumpy platform surrounding it. Its mounds, composed of white geyserite rock, resembled large muffin tops. He bottled up a sample of steaming water from inside its mouth. It might be the only evidence Peale would have of the geyser that rumbled through camp last night.

Then there was a distraction. In the distance, Peale and the others saw puffs of steam belching out of a gray cone. They jogged in for a closer look. Water droplets spurted into the air along with more hiccups of steam. For what seemed

Hayden's party encounters shooting geysers.

an interminable two or three minutes, the men waited, staring at the clamshell-colored cone at the center of the hill.

It was in the location Langford had said it would be, perched at the southern entrance to the basin. But was this it? Was this the gusher that had played so regularly for last year's party—the one that had been named Old Faithful?

Steam belched from the crater, followed by a spray of watery bullets. In a flash, infinite numbers water bubbles

---

Geyser Glee

Some of the early fur trappers feared the steaming, sulfurous geysers, afraid that they were a sign of the devil. Later explorers, including members of the Hayden Expedition, reacted to the jetting geysers with jubilation. They threw up their hats and cheered at the sheer wonder of the natural spectacle.

A gushing Old Faithful geyser.

For some observers, geysers provoked an almost spiritual experience. After watching the massive Giantess Geyser blow hundreds of feet over treetops, one woman declared to her friend, "I'm going to reform."[159]

In the early 1900s, when hotels existed in Yellowstone, hotel staff would alert guests to the location of erupting geysers in the nearby geyser basin. One tourist, Edward Marston, who visited Yellowstone in 1885, described the flurry of activity surrounding one of these news flashes: "A watchman on the look-out shouts 'The Bee-Hive! The Bee-Hive! . . . . and people rush out of their beds wrapped in blankets, or whatever clothing they can find, and off they go."[160]

Watching thundering waters shoot into the sky is a thrilling, once-in-a-lifetime opportunity, which only Yellowstone and a few other places on Earth provide.

Close-up of Old Faithful's crater.

and steam coalesced and came rocketing through the cone. It looked like an upright fire hose, climbing twenty, forty, sixty, eighty feet!

A real, genuine geyser!

"Intense excitement," wrote Hayden later, didn't even begin to describe the group's reaction.[157] Some tore off their hats. Others whooped and hollered as water soared even higher, up to 150 or more feet in the air.

The thrill seemed unavoidable. Years later, a group of tourists who witnessed the geyser "shouted and cheered till out of breath," wrote 1883 visitor Edwin J. Stanley. "Some fired revolvers and guns in the air."[158]

Water sprayed down around Hayden's party, instantly cooling in the air.

Old Faithful gushed for several minutes. Then all of its spewed water rushed down the sides of the hill, forming dozens of small steaming streams that raced toward the Firehole River.

After the eruption, Hayden's men walked up to study the cone. Upon closer examination they could see that what they thought was dingy gray rock actually gleamed with soft colors. Small sinter beads lined to Old Faithful's inner rim. And there were other formations "as delicate as the down on the butterfly's wing."[161]

As the day went on, the party witnessed other geysers. Something always seemed to be bursting or splashing on the hills adjacent to Old Faithful. One was the Grotto. Looking like some lumbering four-legged beast, this geyser spewed water and steam from several openings. It was probably formed when a small stand of trees was flooded heavily by silica-rich waters. The waters hardened around the trunks and formed openings and holes in the rock.

The "prettiest," thought Peale, was the Castle. It had an imposing twenty-five-foot-tall crater that reminded the men of a turret on a castle. It was cracked in many places as if it had once violently exploded. But in looking at the

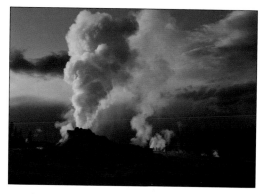
Castle geyser.

An erupting Yellowstone geyser.

shelled wall, it was just as easy to believe, thought Peale, that the Castle had been bombarded by medieval warriors.

There were dozens more, including geysers that inspired names such as Tardy, Beehive, and Spasmodic. Some simmered quietly, others stewed broodingly, while still others gurgled playfully. There were geysers that jetted regularly and others that appeared to follow no particular schedule at all.

In the end, Hayden's men—mostly Peale—documented five hundred springs in this small stretch of the Firehole Valley. The group wished they had more time to explore this dynamic stretch of bubbling earth. And, as Hayden noted, they might even get used to watching columns of hot water burst into the sky.

But they couldn't remain in Yellowstone's great geyser basin any longer. The crew had shed pounds from their bodies and the men were growing increasingly weak. And the news back at camp had only gotten worse.

For the fifth day in a row, they learned, there was no meat. Peale's journal entry for that day hints at their desperation: "Our rapidly diminishing stores [warn] us . . . to turn towards the Lake. We brought provisions for six days . . . reducing ourselves to one biscuit a day."[162]

With a painful hunger chewing at their stomachs, the men tucked themselves in for the night. The moon rose in the sky, coaxing a variety of wild creatures to hunt, sing, and prowl around their camp. In addition to the sparks popping from the fire, the men may have heard yipping coyotes, the squawk of a great horned owl, or the chilling humanlike scream of the mountain lion.

Great horned owl.

At around 10:00 p.m., there was another sound, of water blowing out of a crater. A geyser? They rushed out of their tents. An "immense volume of steam," as Peale described it, billowed up from a nearby hill.[163]

A thick silver column shot up into the moonlit sky. It chugged steadily, reaching a height of at least one hundred feet for several minutes. The sounds were explosive and steady. Years later, one tourist described an erupting geyser as sounding like gunfire, a large number of galloping horses, and a "fearful tornado."[164]

Then, the thundering stopped. The waters ceased erupting and drained into the Firehole River. Some of the men returned to their tents. But Hayden continued to stare.

His patience paid off. Just moments later, an even larger column of white water shot up over the tree tops. It surged. Each burst piggybacked onto the previous one, enabling the spray to climb higher and higher. In the end, Hayden reported back to the party that the geyser has soared a full two hundred feet into the sky.

They called it the Grand Geyser.

Even after most of the men had gone to bed, the Grand Geyser continued to rumble on. Its shock waves made Peale "dream it all over again."[165]

CHAPTER 12
HEADING HOME

All our flour is used and we have to live on meat, coffee and tea.[166]
—Albert Peale, mineralogist in Yellowstone

Hayden's small party had been away from base camp for almost a week now. Even though there was more steaming terrain to explore, the men knew they had no other choice: with rations exhausted, they desperately needed to return to the lake. Luckily someone in the group managed to shoot a rabbit that morning, so each man gobbled down his small portion of rabbit stew. Anything helped fill the emptiness of their stomachs.

Just before leaving the site, Hayden was treated to one last watery spectacle. As if almost on cue, Old Faithful rocketed 150 feet into the sky, holding its steady column of water, Hayden noted, "with the utmost of care."[167] Maybe someday the geologist would get to investigate more of this fascinating valley.

The party headed out, weaving through some of the same clotted pine stands they'd struggled through before. The monotonous scenery made navigation difficult. Jose and Elliott argued over directions, and Elliott stormed off in disgust. Wearied horses froze in their tracks and had to be yanked along by the reins. By sunset, Hayden and Schonburn declared that the party was lost.

A Splashy Name

As they were among the first white men to officially document the Yellowstone area, members of the 1870 Washburn-Langford party earned the privilege of naming many of region's geysers. In the twenty-two hours they spent roaming the geyser basin around Old Faithful, the party saw twelve major geysers in action.

They called one geyser the Castle, because of its forty-foot-tall cone that resembled a tower, or turret, on an aging castle. The "perfect" geyser, according to Langford, which spouted regularly, became known as Old

Faithful. And the one that shot up over two hundred feet in the air and thundered on for more than three hours was aptly called the Giant.

In watching these geysers, the men could hardly contain their excitement. They whooped, hollered, and threw their hats high into the air. And one geyser especially, more than any other, left them spellbound.

This "grand geyser of the world," according to Lieutenant Doane,

An impressive gusher the party didn't see: Lonestar Geyser, a popular "backcountry" geyser located a few miles from Old Faithful.

announced its eruption with a loud sequence of thuds that shook the ground.[168] Massive clouds of steam belched from its crater and surged five hundred feet into the air. Then, a thick column of water shot skyward. Its boiling waters rained back on the earth causing a "thousand hissing sounds." Under the shining sun, the geyser, which was eventually called The Giantess, formed sparkling rainbows in the sky, leaving the whole party "wild with enthusiasm."[169]

They pushed on, planning to camp at the first sight of water, but the group suffered more setbacks. A mule became mired in heavy mud and had to be tediously unloaded, extracted from the muck, then detoured around the offending goo. One of the men was kicked in the ankle. Fortunately, two of his companions—Peale and Hayden—were doctors by training and helped dress the wound. As nightfall neared, the weary and depleted crew finally set up camp near shimmering waters, likely near the shores of today's Lost Lake.

The next morning, after plodding along for another three miles, they finally spied the smoke of a campfire and heard the chatter of their comrades. Hayden's investigation of Yellowstone's geysers had finally come to a successful end.

While the parties were thrilled to see one another and share stories, the mood at camp was hardly upbeat. The men at the lake were famished, too. They had also eaten most of their food supplies. Adams, the survey's assistant botanist, grimly observed, "Starvation was staring us in the face."[170]

The men's camp at Yellowstone Lake.

The rations were made even more stringent until Stevenson could return with more food. That meant that each man was limited to one biscuit and one cup of tea for supper, in addition to whatever other small animals he could catch, kill, and cook.

But there was even more chilling news: the expedition had lost almost half of its military escort while Hayden's crew had been away. Apparently, agitations between railroad surveyors and the Sioux had increased. Sitting Bull, leader of the Sioux, was believed to be planning a full-scale retaliation. Fort Ellis's soldiers had been called back to protect the railroad crews, who were trespassing through Sioux lands. Once again, the US government had sent troops to safeguard the business interests of the millionaire Jay Cooke.

***

Chief Sitting Bull, named Jumping Badger as a child, courageously challenged the landgrab tactics of the Northern Pacific railroad.

The following week Stevenson returned with more supplies, and never were the men more happy to see him. They got warm biscuits again, wrote Peale, "the first in a long time."[171] After a satisfying meal, many of the men in the team were ready to tackle their remaining objective: to map and sketch the rest of Yellowstone Lake.

By now, Thomas Moran and William Henry Jackson had finished their pictures of the lake. As usual, the pair worked separately from the rest of the party, lingering at different spots that they wished to photograph and sketch. The two artists had to wait for the survey scientists to finish their work before they could borrow the boat, a "tiny, frail craft," noted Jackson, which barely supported the photographic supplies he loaded into it: "Any slight squall would have swamped us."[172] Thankfully, he and Moran returned safely with more pictures to add to the Yellowstone portfolio.

Now, he and Moran were setting off toward the geyser basins. Lieutenant Doane, who was heading back to Fort Ellis with the called-upon military escort, was able to help guide them part of the way. Perhaps more than any other of Yellowstone's features, it was Yellowstone's spouting fountains that Moran and Jackson

Great Springs of the Firehole, by Thomas Moran.

needed to capture. A picture would provide indisputable evidence that its geysers really did exist.

As they tramped across the steaming basin, Moran and Jackson were struck by many of the same features that had wowed Hayden, Peale, and the other men. Moran stared at the gaping Great Springs crater. He sketched its sprawling layers and jotted down the names of the colors he saw—yellow, orange, blue. He would swab these in, layer by layer, back at his studio.

Sacred Steam

Little is known about how the early Native peoples in Yellowstone interacted with the region's geysers, hot springs, and vats of splattering mud. Today, archeological and anthropological studies in Yellowstone National Park are providing us with information about how various American Indian tribes used the region.

Descendants of those tribes, many of whom still feel a vital connection to Yellowstone, have been willing to share stories with researchers about how their people used the steaming region.

One Crow man recalled how his mother used pots of steaming mud to "refinish the white buckskin."[174] Another man, a Shoshone, explained a more sacred connection to Yellowstone's strange and natural wonders. "The Indians prayed to the geysers," he said, "because they believed that there were spirits inside them."[175]

An erupting Grotto Geyser. Notice the fine scratches added by Jackson to enhance the appearance of shooting water.

Many years later, viewers of Moran's painting would second-guess the legitimacy of the bright hues. But another government explorer to Yellowstone in 1878 confirmed their accuracy: "The colors," the witness reported, "cannot be exaggerated."[173]

Moran and Jackson journeyed on through the splattering landscape of the Firehole Valley. Jackson made pictures of Castle Geyser and an erupting Old Faithful. But once again, he became frustrated by the limitations of nineteenth-century photography in trying to capture the sheer magnitude of the natural features he was confronted with.

The current wet-plate process allowed plates to be made light-sensitive to only blue light in a spectrum. Consequently, some of the most fantastic images during a geyser eruption—billowing clouds and steam—could not be recorded on the plate. So the wily Jackson improvised yet again. After he took a picture of a geyser, he lightly scratched the glass with small streaks and dashes to help convey the essence of bursting water.

Meanwhile, back at the lake, the rest of the men struggled to complete their work. They were pelted by hailstorms and endured overnight temperatures of 15 degrees Fahrenheit and below. One day, winds were so fierce on the lake that the boat's mast was torn off. Fortunately, by then, Elliott and another man had already sketched the lake's 175 miles of shoreline, completing the final task set out for them.

The men were also rocked by an overnight earthquake. Alarmed and frightened, the night's two guards watched as pine trees swayed, horses sprang to their feet, and birds shot from trees. Earthquakes, triggered by Yellowstone's close-to-the-surface magma, rattled Hayden's expedition a few more times during the remainder of their stay, leading the men to name the affected campsite Earthquake Camp.

What a turbulent finish to their almost six-week trip through Yellowstone. The exploring party had looped around the massive high-altitude lake and was now tromping north. The next major stop was Fort Ellis, and then—after some additional scrambling through the Wyoming Territory—on to Washington, DC, and other points back east.

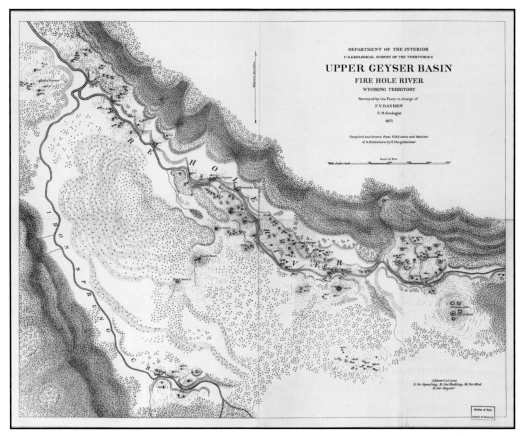

One of the Hayden Expedition's crowning achievements was a map detailing the location of hundreds of hot springs, geysers, and other features in the Upper Geyser Basin.

After logging some of the most thrilling—and harrowing—moments of their careers, the Hayden Expedition had finally completed its ambitious mission. On August 28, just before leaving the Yellowstone Valley, its leader enthusiastically informed Spencer Baird of his survey's success. "We have secured the most important altitudes with accuracy," Hayden proudly relayed. "We have made beautiful charts of all the Hot Spring districts in the valley of the Yellow Stone."[176]

Further, Hayden praised the efforts of his diligent staff, including Henry Elliott, who "sketched all the Craters, the Geysers in motion, the Mud Springs," and William Henry Jackson, who captured Yellowstone's astonishing rarities on more than four hundred glass plate negatives, many a lofty 8 by 10 inches in size.[177] And Schonburn, Hayden added, performed "splendid Topographical work."[178]

By now Hayden was fully convinced of Yellowstone's rare phenomenon. Not only that, but earlier descriptions he'd heard about the region—even Langford's grandiose piece in *Scribner's*—"fell far short of the Truth."[179]

There was one final discovery Hayden's party made before exiting Yellowstone: piles of axed-down trees. They were logs of the lodgepole pine, as straight as today's telephone poles, which grow in dense forests around Old Faithful and its neighboring geyser basin. Two local settlers, caught up in the land-grab fever sweeping the West, planned to use the logs to stake out many of Yellowstone's geysers as their own.

Old Faithful was about to be fenced in.

CHAPTER 13

BACK IN WASHINGTON

The intelligent American will one day point on the map to this remarkable district with the conscious pride that it has not its parallel on the face of the globe.[180]

—Ferdinand Hayden

FALL 1871

Cover of railroad brochure "Where Gush the Geysers."

American newspapers were eagerly awaiting the expedition's return and the findings Hayden and his survey team would bring with them. In a September 18, 1871 article, the *New York Times* wrote that it was holding out for final proof of Yellowstone, one of the "most wonderful tracts of the American continent."[181] As the existence of geysers in the region still seemed preposterous to some, the article included a vivid description by expedition artist and geyser witness Henry Elliott: "I have stood by a crater," he wrote, "and have seen a column of hot boiling water six feet in diameter, ascend with a single bound..."[182] Hayden's official report would provide the remaining details.

By the end of October, Hayden was back in Washington, DC. With much of the nation waiting for information about his recent expedition, he frantically set to work. And so did his team.

Survey members began unpacking the forty-five large crates full of specimens that had been carefully loaded and sent via train to the Smithsonian. There were over one thousand mineral samples to evaluate, including bottles of the strange water that Albert Peale had ladled from Yellowstone's hot springs, mud pots, and geysers. There were also numerous animal skins, bird eggs, preserved reptiles, and insects, as well as hundreds of pressed wildflowers and other plants to organize and describe.

Most of the collection would remain at the Smithsonian Institution for scientific use, while duplicate samples of rocks and other specimens would be sent to universities across the country. Other scientists and staff finished maps, crunched data, and drafted reports that would be tacked on to Hayden's final write-up.

Hayden's Ringlet (*Coenonympha haydenii*), a butterfly discovered in Yellowstone and named for expedition leader Ferdinand Hayden.

Amid the flurry of activity, Hayden received two letters, both of which had ramifications for him and the nation. In one, he learned that his old friend and survey topographer, Anton Schonborn, was dead. The man who'd helped him chart so much of the new frontier had recently struggled with depression and had committed suicide. The personal loss was a blow for Hayden. In addition, he had to pass off all of Schonborn's papers to other government scientists, hoping they could make the detailed maps that Schonborn had envisioned.

The other letter Hayden received was brief and posed a curious question: What did he think of a plan that would preserve the "Great Geyser Basin" of Yellowstone "as a public park forever?"[183]

A public park? The United States had never before protected lands from development, especially for the benefit of the people. A special "grant" to protect the wonders of Yosemite, including its giant sequoia trees, was established in 1864, but that reserve was managed by the state of California. In this era of hungry land grabbing, the idea of a national park seemed as preposterous to many Americans as the existence of boiling fountains.

Something else was odd about the note Hayden read. It was signed by A. B. Nettleton, Jay Cooke's office manager.

Why would a railroad with so much commercial interest in the region be interested in a public park filled with geysers? It boiled down to smart business. The company, well aware of the growing number of get-rich-quick

US mills and development crowding nearby Niagara Falls.

schemes swirling in the steam clouds above Yellowstone, wished to eliminate the competition. Conflicting land claims would be messy and costly. Jay Cooke preferred to limit his dealings with the one entity he'd already proven he could bend to his desires: the government.

Hayden ran with the idea of Yellowstone becoming a government park, but not in the way Cooke had probably hoped. As a geologist, Hayden viewed Yellowstone's resources as ancient works of art. He saw the incoming tide of settlers swarming the region—the squatters at both White Mountain and Old Faithful—and feared Yellowstone's rare curiosities could be lost in the future.

Such one-time kings of the forest were axed for profit and pleasure.

Hayden was also regretful, as other Americans were, of the sad fate of Niagara Falls, a once-beloved national treasure that had been spoiled by greed. By the 1860s, all of the overlooks at the falls on the American side had been staked out by private individuals. Visitors were charged a fee at every one to see the natural wonder (in addition to being hassled by other swindlers). Europeans ridiculed the United States for spoiling its stunning resources. "In Europe," Alexis de Tocqueville wrote, "people talk a great deal about the wilds of America, but the Americans themselves never think about them."[184]

However, there were a growing number of Americans who were dismayed by the country's selfish impulses towards its natural wonders and landscape. John Muir, a Scotsman who spent most of his life rambling across the wilds of America, found deep satisfaction and relaxation in nature. He thought that the late nineteenth century's overworked, money-focused Americans would benefit from escaping to nature, too.

"Climb the mountains and get their good tidings," Muir encouraged his American readers. Then "cares will drop away from you like the leaves of autumn."[185]

John Muir.

"Climb the Mountains: Get Their Good Tidings"

John Muir, a man who nearly lost his vision—and his life—would eventually cast his eyes upon the beautiful Yosemite Valley and declare it "the grandest of all the special temples of Nature."[186]

Muir, a Scotsman by birth, delighted in hiking in the mountains and observing wild nature. But as a young man working in a carriage factory, he suffered a serious accident that left him blind and fearful that he would never see again. After several weeks passed, however, Muir regained his eyesight and with fresh zeal decided to pursue his life's passion: exploring nature. But shortly thereafter, bad luck struck again when on a hike from Indiana to the Gulf of Mexico, Muir became gravely ill with malaria and almost died.

Thankfully for us, this geologist, author, and nature lover survived the episode and went on to help establish Yosemite and Sequoia National Parks. His passionate writings helped persuade Americans to reconsider the value of wilderness—that being outdoors could reinvigorate body and spirit. As Muir once wrote, "Thousands of tired, nerve-shaken, over-civilized people are beginning to find out that going to the mountains is going home."[187]

The People Need Green Space

This is what Frederick Law Olmstead, an eloquent author, conservationist, and public park planner, argued. Growing up in the country at a time of rapid growth and industrialization, Olmstead worried that society's fast pace was wearing down Americans. This was especially true, he believed, for working- and middle-class individuals who couldn't afford luxurious travel or access to the private wooded estates that were so popular among that era's wealthy.

At the end of the workday, people need a tranquil place to escape to, Olmstead wrote, "where they may stroll for an hour, seeing, hearing, and feeling nothing of the bustle and jar of the streets."[188]

Frederick Law Olmsted, architect and park advocate.

Olmsted advocated for the establishment of parks—from small and large city parks to extensive wilderness preserves, including Yosemite National Park. The insightful land planner was also co-creator of New York's beloved Central Park.

Olmstead believed in the restorative value of nature and how saving it was good for the nation. But just as important, he stated, was making park and recreational access as democratic as possible. He feared that without government intervention, the "very few, very rich" would lay claim to America's most magnificent scenery, causing "the mass of the people" to be shut out from those glorious places.[189]

With his deep appreciation for green space and strong democratic principles, Frederick Law Olmstead was an important architect of the United States' national park concept.

It was Muir and a group of fellow conservationists who, in 1864, had rallied to save Yosemite Valley and its giant sequoia trees, which were being hacked at for timber and sheer novelty.

If Hayden was to do the same for Yellowstone, he needed to act quickly. For the remainder of the year, he labored over his five-hundred-plus page report on Yellowstone, and prodded his colleagues to finish theirs. He selected several of Elliott's sketches—of mountain peaks, splashing mud pots, and geyser cones—to illustrate the report's pages.

No evidence, however, would be as compelling as Jackson's photographs. Hayden summoned the photographer to help the effort, and Jackson responded enthusiastically, even though that meant leaving his very pregnant wife who was now staying with Jackson's family in New York. Hayden was also tasked with writing two articles about the wonders of Yellowstone—one for the popular press and another for a scientific journal. Despite his pressed schedule, the determined Hayden also squeezed in a wedding—his own. He and longtime fiancée Emma Woodruff were finally married in November.

In the meantime, Jay Cooke wanted confirmation from his men in the field that the proposed park plan was still in his company's best interests. He wrote to his top engineer working out of the Montana Territory and asked if the creation of a Yellowstone park would conflict with the railroad's land grant. If not, the company needed to act "speedily," Cooke wrote, "or squatters and claimants will go in there, and we can probably deal much better with the government . . . than with individuals."[190]

CHAPTER 14
FOR THE PEOPLE

In a few years this region will be a place of resort for all classes of people from all portions of the world.
　—Ferdinand Hayden, advocating for the passage of the "Yellowstone Park Bill"

WINTER 1872

Since Congress and the American people could not easily get to Yellowstone, Hayden did his best to "bring" the remarkable region to them. He arranged for dazzling public displays of specimens his survey team had gathered in Yellowstone to be installed at the US Capitol and the Smithsonian. Alongside chunks of geyser rock and other mineral samples, he also exhibited some of Moran's sketches

Hayden's men in awe of an erupting Old Faithful geyser.

and vivid watercolors to give life and color to the exhibit's artifacts.[191] Jackson's black-and-white photos were circulated among key congressmen who could be influential in helping realize Hayden's goal of preserving the Yellowstone region.

In mid-January, Senator Samuel C. Pomeroy from Kansas tried to get a vote on the bill that would establish Yellowstone as a public park. He explained how the nation's official geologist had confirmed the area's "great geysers" and "waterspouts."[192] A few senators had questions, though. How many square miles would it be? Did the tract contain any valuable agricultural or mining resources?[193]

Pomeroy told them that Hayden had recommended a size of forty square miles for the park in order to include all of Yellowstone's thermal wonders. Pomeroy also assured the senators that the region's high altitude made it unfit for farming.

Even after urging his colleagues to act quickly because of the encroaching settlers, Pomeroy still couldn't get a vote. The matter was tabled until the following week. That's when Senator Cornelius Cole from California announced his objections. "I have grave doubts," he told the room, "about the propriety of passing this bill." He was skeptical that any harm could come to Yellowstone if squatters sought claims there. "The geysers will remain," he insisted, "no matter where the ownership of the land may be."[194]

Senator Lyman Trumbull from Illinois disagreed. His family had direct knowledge of Yellowstone: Trumbull's son Walter had been a member of the 1870 Langford-Washburn party. The young man had witnessed the region's wonders as well as its eager settlers. Private development in Yellowstone, Trumbull argued, would benefit rich and powerful interests and exclude the vast majority of people from getting to see "the most wonderful geysers on the face of the earth." If Congress didn't act, the senator said, a profit-seeking individual could "plant himself across the only path that leads to these wonders, and charge every man that passes . . . a fee."[195]

Thanks to the Hayden Expedition's words and imagery, and the diligence of Senators Pomeroy and Trumbull, the act to safeguard Yellowstone passed the US Senate on January 30, 1872. Montana's *Helena Daily Herald* praised the nation's foresight: "It will be a park worthy of the Great Republic."[196]

***

But not everyone was impressed with the bold new idea of sealing off hundreds of thousands of acres of wilderness to create a public park for the nation's citizens to enjoy. Once settlers in the Yellowstone region learned the news of the bill's passage in the Senate, some began to speak out loudly against it. On February 1, the two squatters at Yellowstone's White Mountain (today's Mammoth Hot Springs) initiated a petition in Bozeman's *Avant Courier*. They demanded that a provision be inserted in the park bill that would allow them to pursue their business operations on White Mountain's pearly terraces without repercussion.

Other settlers, too, demanded free reign in Yellowstone. As far as they were concerned, the land should be open to development and free enterprise. Why should lawmakers miles away in Washington, DC, decide the area's fate? One man, who frequented the bathing pools at White Mountain, was plotting to pave a road across Yellowstone. He planned to charge visitors a fee to use it. Another local—the man who had rescued Truman Everts, the lost member of the Langford-

Washburn Expedition—had already built a toll bridge in the northern part of the Yellowstone region. Gold hunters used it to access nearby streams and rivers and he made a nice profit.

One of Montana's local papers, Helena's *Rocky Mountain Gazette,* spoke for the angered locals. The paper, it stated, is "opposed to any scheme," which keeps Yellowstone in "perpetual solitude." Individual settlers, it argued, should be allowed to open up the Yellowstone country.[197]

That February, another publication was drawing readers' attention to the topic of the Yellowstone bill. It was the *Scribner's* article that Moran had promised to illustrate upon his return from the West. Even though he was already working at a frenetic pace, writing reports and lobbying members of Congress, Hayden agreed to write the article to accompany Moran's mesmerizing pictures. In poetic fashion, Hayden recounted his team's journey through the land of geologic marvels.

At the end of the article, he urged Congress to act immediately on the park bill:

"Why will not Congress at once pass a law," Hayden wrote, "setting it as a great public park for all time to come . . . ?"[198]

Castle Geyser, Upper Geyser Basin, by Thomas Moran.

Around the same time, one of Hayden's closest colleagues and allies in the effort to save Yellowstone received a startling blow. Jackson was stunned to learn that his wife Mollie had died in childbirth. The child, a daughter, was likely born premature and lived only a short while as well. For the rest of his life, Jackson struggled with the pain and guilt of having not been at his wife's side. "These are matters about which," he wrote many years later, "even now, I can write no more."[199]

Still indomitable, Jackson soldiered on. He continued making reproductions of his Yellowstone images. Hayden wrote inspiring captions for the images—of steaming terraces, spurting fountains, and towering rock spires—and then had the images bound into attractive books that were distributed to members of Congress.

Another *Scribner's* author, Nathaniel Langford, was also busy advocating for Yellowstone while Congress debated the bill. Four hundred copies of his original *Scribner's* article were placed on the desks of every congressmen. Langford and Hayden lobbied extensively, personally visiting all members of Congress to try to sway their opinion—and vote. As one historian later noted, likely no bill before Congress had ever been so thoroughly canvassed.

Hayden realized his goliath five-hundred-page report would not be completed in time to have an impact on the current debate in the House, so he hurriedly drafted a shorter synopsis and urgent call to action. In this special report, dated February 27, he spoke plainly and passionately about what would happen if Congress didn't act:

"If this bill fails to become a law . . . the vandals who are now waiting to enter into this wonderland will, in a single season, despoil beyond recovery, these remarkable curiosities."[200] Such resources belonged to all Americans, he added, and should be "as free as the air or the water."[201]

Hayden couldn't have been more right. At that very moment, another enterprising settler, Matthew McGuirk, was getting ready to file his own claim to White Mountain Hot Springs. His claim, separate from the two other squatters', included the portion of White Mountain's springs that rushed into the Gardiner River. He planned to call his development McGuirk's Medicinal Springs.

Congressman Henry L. Dawes, who advocated establishing Yellowstone National Park.

The American Buffalo: A Yellowstone Rescue

At one time America's Great Plains were blackened with buffalo. In their massive migrations, tens of thousands of the animals would roam in unison, reminding photographer William H. Jackson of a "moving carpet."[202] Their dense herds clogged railroad tracks and brought passenger trains to a standstill, sometimes delaying travel for hours.

A buffalo stampede along the Oregon Trail.

But by the end of the nineteenth century, few of the majestic beasts remained. They were hunted ruthlessly—slaughtered for their hides, horns, and sometimes just for their tongues, which were considered a trophy by some hunters. Their skulls were ground into fertilizers to enrich newly created farmlands. The bison's destruction was even endorsed by the US government, which tried to eject Plains Indian tribes from valuable lands by depriving the Natives of a vital food source and sacred symbol.

Slaughtered bison.

By 1901, America's population of free-roaming bison had been decimated, with only a few dozen thought to remain. Thankfully, Yellowstone, which by then had become a national park, harbored an estimated twenty-five animals. Park managers, concerned that America's buffalo would be wiped out permanently, supplemented those last remaining animals with buffalo raised on ranches. Notably, it was local American Indian tribes who donated many of those animals.

Eventually the bison interbred and the herd size flourished. Today, between four and five thousand bison freely roam the park—a number that still pales in comparison to the hundreds of thousands of animals that once ranged freely across America's West.

Bison are well adapted to Yellowstone's boiling features.

The clock was ticking. The House had been sitting on their version of the Yellowstone bill since January. Hayden ramped up his efforts. He visited with Congressman Henry L. Dawes, a longtime supporter of Hayden's scientific trips out West. When budget concerns threatened to hamper the park bill, Hayden promised not to ask for any additional appropriations for his survey work for the next several years.

Finally, thanks largely to the powerful influence of Representative Dawes, Congress voted 115 to 65 in favor of the Yellowstone park bill. The Hayden Expedition's lush artwork, persuasive reports, and displays of curious specimens also played a major role in helping the bill get passed into law.

On March 1, 1872, President Ulysses Grant signed the bill into law. Yellowstone at last belonged to the people.

The nation had saved its Wonderland just in time. McGuirk's land claim (declaring his intent to convert White Mountain into a "medicinal" springs) was dated only eight days later.

★★★

A strange group of forces had convened to create Yellowstone National Park. Surprisingly, a desire for money, power, and even fame (as in the case of Ferdinand Hayden) all played a part. And, just like today, political connections proved vital.

William H. Jackson continued to make pictures well into his nineties.

But what ultimately saved Yellowstone was a growing concern about the fate of the nation's last great wild spaces. America's relationship with its vast and rugged lands had evolved. Instead of fear, we started to feel fascination towards the dark, mysterious woods. We discovered that in addition to material resources, we could also extract personal joy and satisfaction from the land. This fresh thinking ushered in a new idea—the national park idea—which has now become one of the United States' most celebrated exports to the rest of the world.

Hayden, who had been one of the park's most enthusiastic promoters, was so enchanted with the region that he returned to Yellowstone the next year, along with former survey members James Stevenson, Albert Peale, and William Jackson. Albert Peale would always be known as the first scientist to catalog Yellowstone's myriad hot springs and other geothermal marvels.

William Jackson, who lived to the ripe age of ninety-nine, became one of the premier photographers in the American West. He made the most of the era's

Thomas Moran's glowing masterpiece, *Grand Canyon of the Yellowstone.*

A Painting for the People

As soon as Hayden's expedition returned east, Thomas Moran got to work on his Yellowstone paintings. The region's pastel-hued canyon was his first subject. The only way Moran believed he could do the sweeping scenery justice was to paint it on a twelve-foot-long canvas.

For reference, Moran drew upon his numerous sketches, on William H. Jackson's clear photographs, and on his memory—a virtual catalog full of vivid snapshots. He carefully daubed on the elusive colors that he had earlier feared would be impossible to render: the soft pinks, reds, and gaudy yellows.

The resulting oil painting, which was revealed in New York City on May 2, 1872, two months after President Ulysses Grant declared Yellowstone a national park, was considered a masterpiece. Hayden attended the debut, testifying to Moran's scientific accuracy.

When *Scribner's* editor Richard Watson Gilder, who was also a friend of Moran's, saw the oversized painting, he declared: "When I think of his carrying that immense canvas across his brain so long, I wonder that he didn't go through the door sidewise, and call people to look out when they came near."[203]

Congress was so impressed by the painting that they purchased Moran's *Grand Canyon of Yellowstone* to hang in the US Capitol—the first landscape painting to ever grace the walls of the building.

Thomas Moran with impressive catch of fish.

Thomas Moran had achieved his boyhood goal. Thanks largely to his Yellowstone paintings, the artist became one of America's most celebrated landscape painters. In turn, the man who signed his name Thomas "Yellowstone" Moran went on to excite generations of Americans about the grandeur of their western lands.

clumsy photographic capabilities and, luckily for us, documented incredible scenery and cultures that have since faded from that part of our country.

Two months after the Yellowstone park bill passed, Thomas Moran's enormous seven- by twelve-foot masterpiece, *Grand Canyon of the Yellowstone*, debuted before a mystified audience in New York City. The images he'd toiled over while clinging to the edges of cliffs were finally complete. The work helped establish him as a major American landscape painter.

As for the Northern Pacific Railroad, its tracks would never run through current-day Yellowstone. Jay Cooke's company, which was heavily invested in the project, was unable to sell enough bonds to pay for it. That era's economic depression, the Panic of 1873, added to his woes, and Cooke was forced to declare bankruptcy.

The vulnerable wilds of Yellowstone had dodged a bullet. And throughout its history, the park, like all national parks, has continued to face challenges: habitat loss, dwindling genetic diversity, invasive plants and animals, and climate change. The next generation of park stewards will need to draw on the same inventiveness and foresight as those early park planners in 1872 to ensure that America's special places will remain wild for centuries to come.

EPILOGUE
OUR BEST IDEA

A very great vision is needed and the man who has it must follow it as the eagle seeks the deepest blue of the sky.

—Crazy Horse, Oglala Lakota Sioux

Bald eagle.

When the Yellowstone bill was passed in 1872, it was the first time that the United States had publicly put aside its selfish impulses to save a stretch of extraordinary land. It did this, astonishingly, despite the nation's deep appetite for gold, silver, coal, timber, and a host of other raw resources.

The bill also marked the first time that a large tract of exceptional property—choice real estate, you might say—was saved *not* for kings, lords, and tycoons—but for ordinary people. For centuries, the best lands, from fastidiously manicured gardens to sprawling hunting preserves, were typically reserved only

The arch welcoming all visitors to Yellowstone National Park (from a vintage Frank J. Haynes postcard).

for the elite. In 1872, America changed all that, and, consistent with its democratic principles, declared that places like Yellowstone should be set apart for the "benefit and enjoyment of the people" (as the park's current legislation states).

Given this unique innovation—a perfect blend of conservation and democracy—the nation was applauded around the world. Europeans, who had before criticized the nation for

Inscription that appears on the Roosevelt Arch at the northern entrance to Yellowstone National Park.

exploiting its natural assets, now praised the United States for having invented an idea that was ingenious and soon to be emulated across the globe. A British ambassador to the United States was said to have called it the "best idea" America ever had.[204] Ireland's Earl of Dunraven praised the country for what he called a "free gift to man."[205]

Even better, since 1872, more than 130 countries—from Argentina and Guatemala, to New Zealand and South Africa—have copied America and established national parks of their own.

The idea of a national park is continually evolving. There have been shortcomings and ignorance along the way. Shortly after Yellowstone became a national park, the people who had lived there for generations, the Sheepeaters, were essentially forced to leave their sacred and ancestral lands.

Furthermore, Yellowstone's bison, elk, and deer continued to be hunted until further laws made it illegal to kill wildlife within the park. And the wolf, a vital predator in Yellowstone, was slaughtered mercilessly until the 1930s, when biologists finally began to understand its important role in the larger ecosystem.

We've learned many lessons—but have many more to work through.

In the meantime, one of the best ways to support your National Parks is to learn about them. There are fifty-eight of these spectacular places in the United States. Visit www.nps.gov for information on all of America's national parks.

And most importantly of all, get out and experience the parks' weird and wild beauty for yourself. The national parks belong to you.

Map of the US National Parks

IT'S ALIVE!

A GUIDE TO YELLOWSTONE'S HYDROTHERMAL FEATURES

A volcanic giant sleeps under Yellowstone, breathing life into one of the most diverse biomes on Earth.

In 1872, Yellowstone's geysers, hot springs, and other scorching marvels captured the nation's imagination—and its consciousness. At that time, most Americans had never seen or even read about such strange, gushing beauties. And neither had members of Congress, who were ultimately motivated to save Yellowstone as a great public park for all time.

Yellowstone's leaping mud pots and turquoise hot springs the size of swimming pools certainly captivated Ferdinand Hayden and his team of brawny sleuths. Using basic tools—thermometers, crude chemistry, and even the surfaces of their mouths—Hayden's group were the first scientists to document the region's spitting cauldrons and jetting fountains. The men returned home with more questions than answers, but still, Hayden's crew knew they'd encountered something extraordinary.

Enthralled by its quirky boilers, Hayden returned to Yellowstone two more times, in 1872 and 1878. Countless other scientists have followed him. Each has added to our understanding of Yellowstone's peculiar landscape and the impressive array of life forms that depend on it—from the tiny microbes that flourish in its sizzling pools to the herds of snorting bison that soak up its vital steam in the winter.

And one force, more than any other, powers this rich habitat: a strange and ancient fire raging beneath the region's surface.

An 1871 Yellowstone expedition member peers into the fuming Dragon's Mouth Spring.

PLUTO'S DOMAIN

Imagine standing in Yellowstone's Firehole Valley on a stretch of bleached white rock. Old Faithful spews nearby. Warm steam cushions your face. The smell of rotten eggs invades your nose.

But what you *can't* see, touch, or smell is the massive underground furnace just three to four miles below your feet: a blob of red-hot, partially melted rock.

Stand elsewhere on Earth, including your own backyard, and a similar pocket of heat would take fifty or more miles to reach the surface.

Scientists know about this semi-molten pocket because of three-dimensional pictures they've constructed of the interior of the Earth. Using seismographs (or seismometers), which are instruments that

Old Faithful geyser.

measure the force of earthquakes, geologists can tell which of the Earth's layers are dense and which are loose and fluid.

It's the speed of seismic waves that makes all the difference. The waves race through hard, dense layers of rock, while they creep sluggishly through jelly-like, molten layers. The semi-molten layer just a few miles below Yellowstone is called a magma chamber. As hot as 1500 degrees Fahrenheit, this underground oven is also called a pluton, named after the Greek god of the underworld, Pluto. But there's a larger, more intense source of heat feeding the chamber. It originates deeper, at least fifty miles down. Known as the Yellowstone hot spot, it draws some of its heat from the Earth's innermost blazing layer: its core.

A sprawling 300 to 500 miles wide, the Yellowstone hot spot consists of flaming red-orange rock. About thirty hot spots are known to exist across the world. They're formed when weak spots, or fissures, in the Earth allow superheated, molten rock to rise up from the core. Light-weight and excitable, such superheated molecules can't help but bob upward—similar to the way the blobs in a lava lamp bubble to the top.

BLOW!

Over the course of Yellowstone's history, these semi-molten blobs rose until they reached the overlying hard granite layer that makes up much of the Earth's outer crust. Given their intense heat, these blazing masses melted portions of the granite crust, creating the magma chamber that roils beneath Yellowstone today.

Granite, just like the speckled countertops you see in kitchens and bathrooms, is composed of different-colored minerals, including feldspar, mica, and quartz. Because each mineral has its own melting temperature, the magma chamber sitting beneath Yellowstone is a combination of both hard and semi-molten rock (think of the dual consistency of gel-filled hard candies).

At different times in Yellowstone's history, the heat bubbling up from the hot spot became hotter and more intense. This added heat, like cranking up the burner

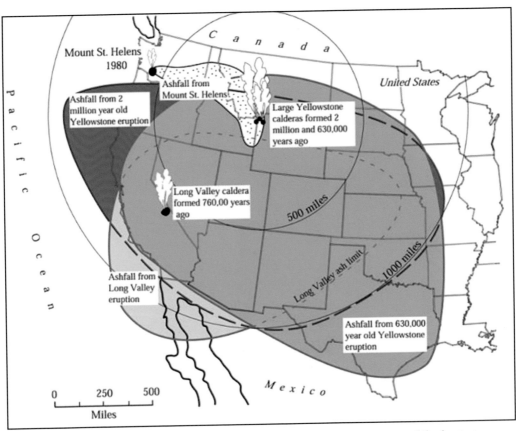

Volcanic eruptions have occurred throughout North America's history. Two of the largest were caused by Yellowstone's volcanic system.

on a gas stove, caused the magma chamber over top to burble more fiercely. As the heat intensified, the magma chamber swelled and bulged, putting incredible pressure on the layer of crust on top of it. Like the heavy lid on a pressure cooker, the rigid roof of that overlying crust blocked the energy surging below. With no way to vent its terrific power, the magma chamber, pushed to the limit, exploded.

Yellowstone, in effect, is a super volcano. And over the course of its history, Yellowstone's super volcano has blown at least three times. Based on the depth and location of erupted volcanic material in the greater Yellowstone region, scientists estimate that such massive eruptions occurred roughly 2 million, 1.3 million, and 640,000 years ago.

It's hard to fathom the power and scope of such an explosion. Hot rock and magma would have rocketed into the sky at supersonic speeds. Ash would have pelted the ground, raining down over half of the North American continent. Clouds of gases, including aerosols, would have flooded the atmosphere, causing "volcanic winters" that chilled the planet for years.

A topographic map of the Greater Yellowstone Region, including its most recent caldera, outlined in red.

As the Yellowstone volcano ejected tons of material, it collapsed in on itself, swallowing up the region's mountains, rivers, and other major landforms. The most recent volcanic eruption triggered a collapse of about 1,000 feet, creating a caldera (the Spanish word for cauldron) that measures about 45 by 30 miles wide.

It's this vast volcanic scar that Ferdinand Hayden spied in 1871. And, of course, in the blink of time since then, visitors to Yellowstone can still see the rim of that ancient eruption today. The heat beneath the caldera continues to simmer, powering the geothermal curiosities found in current-day Yellowstone.

But is another super-eruption coming anytime soon? ("Soon" in geologic time can mean tens, to hundreds, to even thousands of years from now!)

It's highly unlikely. Instead, scientists expect more immediate rumbling events to include local steam explosions and lava flows—which would be disruptive, yes, but not catastrophic.

In the meantime, scientists are watching the Yellowstone hot spot breathe, gently rising and falling like a slumbering underground giant. They study the geysers and hot springs closely, looking for changes in their temperatures and patterns of eruption. They also track the region's frequent earthquakes. Yellowstone is certain to provide major signs if it's about to blow again anytime soon!

GURGLE OR GUSH?

"Bubblers." "Mud Puffs." "Nature's soda fountains." Yellowstone's ten thousand steaming wonders have been called many things, but today, scientists use specific terms to describe and classify them.

The three main types of thermal features found in Yellowstone and in other thermal regions across the globe are: hot springs, geysers, and steam vents, also known as fumaroles.

So what makes one feature quietly simmer while another boisterously blows? It depends on three main elements: water, rock, and the type and availability of underground "plumbing."

Water determines how fluid a feature will be. A steam vent, a small, chugging chimney on the surface of the ground, has access to underground heat but little to no access to water. These features, also known as fumaroles—after the Latin word *fumus*, which means smoke—can eject hot steam so thunderously that they can be heard miles away.

Fumaroles, or steaming vents, are among the hottest hydrothermal features in Yellowstone.

Ojo Caliente Spring, meaning "hot eye" in Spanish.

Water availability depends on recent weather and the amount of rain and snow that has seeped down into the ground. It also depends on a method of delivery. A large network of channels exists beneath Yellowstone. Abundant earthquakes in the region, which are triggered by the fuming hot spot beneath the region, rattle the Earth's crust and cause it to crack. These underground cracks act as pipes that can shuttle water horizontally and vertically.

When these pipes are wide enough, they carry water easily and gently to the Earth's surface, creating a hot spring. When the pipes are constricted, however, pressure builds. Trapped water bubbles up violently against cinched spots. When the water finally releases itself, the superheated load rockets through a narrowing in the ground—like taking the cap off a shaken-up bottle of soda. The result is an erupting geyser.

It's one such constriction—about four inches wide—that makes one of the world's most famous geysers, Old Faithful, possible.

Geysers also require hard, temperature-tough rock. The rock layer beneath Old Faithful and its neighbors is rich in silica, a durable white substance that seals underground channels when it hardens. This creates an ideal plumbing material for zipping hot water back and forth underground.

Over time, as a geyser erupts regularly, silica is deposited on the ground around the opening,

Giant geyser, a cone-type geyser.

creating a variety of shapes—from small beads, to large cauliflower-shaped mounds, to massive, car-sized cones. And because silica is the main element found in opal, many of these formations appear shimmery or translucent.

PLOPPING PASTELS

In contrast to geysers and hot springs, the substrate beneath Yellowstone's mud pot fields consists mostly of clay. These gooey particles were deposited by an earlier Yellowstone Lake that once covered a larger portion of the present-day park.

Hot water and steam, burbling up from the magma chamber, form acids that react with the rock. For months, years, centuries, or even longer, this scalding water and the chemicals it contains break down the surrounding rock into clay particles that are as fine as chalk dust. This marathon boil also yields a variety of colors, both beautiful and ghastly—from pink, yellow, and pale orange, to black, gray, and a split-pea-soup color.

Close-up of Fountain Paint Pots.

Reminding earlier explorers of pots of boiling mush, Yellowstone's mud pots are also impacted greatly by the availability of water. In spring and early summer, when snowpack on higher mountains melts and drains into the valleys, mud features are typically slushy and watery. By late summer, they usually dry out and form deep cracks. Yet they still ooze the sewer-like smell of hydrogen sulfide, a gas originating deep in the Earth that's often associated with volcanoes and thermal features.

UNEXPECTED SURVIVORS

The uppermost temperature for life was believed to be 162 degrees Fahrenheit (or 72 degrees Centigrade). That's what scientists thought, anyway, prior to the summer of 1966, when microbiologist Thomas Brock, in scooping up some pale-pink threads from a blazing Yellowstone hot spring, made a discovery that ultimately stunned the scientific world.

Heat-loving bacteria similar to those collected by microbiologist Thomas Brock in 1966.

The sample Brock collected, it turned out, contained tiny organisms capable of surviving in water as hot as *176 degrees Fahrenheit!* Called *Thermus aquaticus*, or *Taq* for short, this temperature-tough microbe—which resembles miniature pretzel rods under a microscope—was the most heat-tolerant organism ever to be found on Earth.

Since Brock's breakthrough discovery, numerous other heat-loving microorganisms, or thermophiles, have been discovered in Yellowstone. Some have proven to be even more heat-tolerant than *Taq*.

Peering into hot pools teeming with these impressive microorganisms is like looking through a window into ancient Earth. Thermophiles like *Taq* are descendents of the earliest life forms on Earth, capable of withstanding an otherwise brutal world of intense heat and acid. Such harsh conditions likely prevailed on our planet four billion years ago, long before oxygen-dependent organisms ever existed.

Now researchers are sleuthing other harsh and volatile places for life, including Mars, which may also harbor Yellowstone-like microbes.

VIVID CARPET

Pale yellow. Orange Creamsicle. Caramel brown. Each of these colors, often seen radiating out from the bright-blue nucleus of a boiling hot spring, is associated with a specific thermophile.

Lighter colored mats of microorganisms—creamy white to yellow—are generally associated with higher temperatures. Meanwhile, darker, dingier mats are associated with organisms thriving on the lower end of the spectrum. (But even these microbes are heat-tough; they can thrive in temperatures hotter than your average 104-degree-Fahrenheit hot tub!)

The colorful pigments of thermophiles serve as protection against the sun. The orange-colored mats that swirl around the 370-foot-wide Grand Prismatic

A mat of heat-loving microbes encircling a hot spring.

Thermophiles create a blazing carpet of color.

Spring are comprised of millions of bacteria that produce carotenoids—protective yellow, orange, and red pigments that are also produced by plants such as carrots.

HOT WATER WILDLIFE

As these heat-loving microbial mats grow denser and thicker, comprising billions of individual microorganisms, they begin to form communities that can support an extensive variety of life. For instance, certain flies, like the ephydrid (pronounced "ef-id-rid"), a non-biting insect, live most of their short two-week lives on warm algae mats that thrive in the hot-water channels running from hot springs and geysers.

These flies are so closely adapted to their warm algae home that they have evolved exquisite mechanisms for protecting the pink-orange eggs they deposit in the warm goo. For instance, to avoid predators the flies lay their eggs inside tiny air bubbles, which can then be injected more deeply into the warm algae mats and out of harm's way.

But the flies can't dodge all the hungry creatures waiting in the

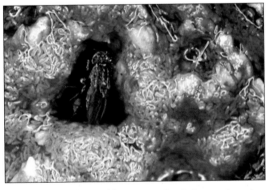

An ephydrid fly and larvae embed themselves in a mat of heat-loving bacteria.

wings. Poised at the hot pool's edges are spiders that will dash quickly onto hot microbial mats for a chance to snack on the clusters of pink-orange eggs. The eggs are also a favorite snack of killdeer and other birds, as well as of dragonflies, predatory flies, wasps, and mites.

A grazing elk seems unfazed by a nearby geyser.

The warmth of Yellowstone's geysers and hot pools sustain much larger animals, too. During the region's frigid winters, with subzero temperatures and several feet of snowpack, thermal regions draw numerous deer, elk, bison, coyotes, wolves, and bears.

With less snow in these areas, elk and bison have an easier time finding grasses to eat. Their hoof prints pock Yellowstone's thermal areas. Weary members, weakened by the harsh winter, then draw in meat-eating predators such as wolves and bears.

In the spring, whole carcasses are often found around the edges of hot springs, evidence that a winter death—and feast—has taken place. Such a vital food source nourishes wolves, coyotes, hawks, badgers, and pine martens—as well as later diners, including squirrels and chipmunks that gnaw on bleached animal bones for needed calcium.

A ONE-OF-A-KIND LABORATORY

Yellowstone is the "greatest laboratory . . . on the surface of the globe," wrote Lieutenant Gustavus Doane in 1870. And because the region was preserved as a national park more than 140 years ago, scientists can study this vast and still-wild ecosystem today, a rarity on our increasingly crowded planet.

With the help of solid science and thoughtful management, we can maintain this sprawling outdoor laboratory. By doing so, we will ensure that future scientists, like you, have a chance to study its astonishing inhabitants and processes, some of which are still mysterious and unknown.

Riverside geyser.

Even if you can't get to Yellowstone any time soon, you can watch the Old Faithful geyser erupt in real time by visiting the National Park Service webcam found at www.nps.gov/yell/learn/photosmultimedia/webcams.htm.

To learn the latest about Yellowstone's sleeping volcano, visit the Yellowstone Volcano Observatory online at volcanoes.usgs.gov/yvo/.

And for many other exciting discoveries made by scientists in Yellowstone today, visit www.nps.gov/yell/learn/yellowstone-science.htm.

ACKNOWLEDGMENTS

It would be impossible to accomplish any big goal, including writing a book, without the encouragement of friends and family. Special thanks to my former editor, Linda Tokarz, for prodding me to write after I left full-time work to raise my daughter. I'm indebted to her for her friendship, mentorship, and willingness to look over those *very* rough first drafts.

Thanks to my current editor, Julie Matysik, for her keen eye and perspective, and for providing me with this incredible opportunity. And deep gratitude to my dynamo of an agent, Carrie Pestritto, whose enthusiasm for this project was the spark that helped turn a dream into a reality.

Thanks to Roger Anderson, who opened the door for me professionally by giving me my first job in Yellowstone, and to Yellowstone National Park historian Lee Whittlesey and Jessica Gerdes, both of the Yellowstone Research Library, for their helpfulness and support. Many thanks to Jacob B. Lowenstern, Scientist-in-Charge at the Yellowstone Volcano Observatory, for reviewing text related to Yellowstone's restless volcanic system. I'd also like to gratefully acknowledge author and historian Marlene Deahl Merrill, who carefully researched and transcribed two previously unpublished journals from the 1871 Yellowstone expedition. The thrilling details contained in those men's personal accounts and published in Merrill's *Yellowstone and the Great West: Journals, Letters, and Images from the 1871 Hayden Expedition* were indispensible to me.

A very special and heartfelt thanks to my parents for their constant support and love, and for so many years ago loading my sister and me up in the family van and driving us cross-country to see Yellowstone. That introduction shaped my passions and the course of my life. Thanks, too, to my sister for always rooting me on.

Finally, I thank my husband, whose devotion, support, and patience has no parallel. Yellowstone will always be a special place to us, and I am deeply grateful, especially to him and our daughter, for having had the chance to write about it.

And, my dear Ella, thank you for letting Mommy write. This book is for you.

ENDNOTES

Prologue:

1 Tilden, Freeman. *The National Parks*. New York: Alfred A. Knopf, 1970: 97–98.
2 Langford, Nathaniel. "The Wonders of the Yellowstone." *Scribner's Monthly*. (May 1871): 2.
3 Ibid, 17.
4 Merrill, Marlene Deahl. *Yellowstone and the Great West: Journals, Letters, and Images from the 1871 Hayden Expedition*. Lincoln, Nebraska: University of Nebraska Press, 1999: 10.
5 Chittenden, Hiram Martin. *Yellowstone National Park*. Stanford, California: Stanford University Press, 1933: 48.
6 LaSalle, Michael E. *Emigrants on the Overland Trail: The Wagon Trains of 1848*. Kirksville, Missouri: Truman State University Press, 2011: 5.
7 Freeman, 98.

Chapter 1:

8 Linderman, Frank B. *Plenty Coups: Chief of the Crows*. Lincoln, Nebraska: University of Nebraska Press, 1962: 227.
9 Haines, Aubrey L. *The Yellowstone Story: A History of Our First National Park, Volume One*. Yellowstone National Park, Wyoming: Yellowstone Library and Museum Association, 1977: 4.
10 Merrill, 10.
11 Nabokov, Peter, and Lawrence Loendorf. "American Indians and Yellowstone National Park." Report prepared for National Park Service, Yellowstone Center for Resources, Yellowstone National Park, 2002.
12 Haines, 26.
13 Ibid., 26.
14 Brands, H.W. *The Age of Gold: The California Gold Rush and the New American Dream*. New York: Doubleday, 2002.
15 Waitley, Douglas. *William Henry Jackson: Framing the Frontier*. Missoula, Montana: Mountain Press, 1999: 78.

16   Zweig, Jason. "Business News, 1889: For Mark Twain Finance Is No Laughing Matter." *The Wall Street Journal*, (July 7, 2014).

17   Barsness, Larry. *Gold Camp: Alder Gulch and Virginia City, Montana*. New York: Hastings House, 1962.

18   Nabokov and Loendorf: 173.

19   Ibid., 173.

Chapter 2:

20   Jackson, William Henry. *Time Exposure: The Autobiography of William Henry Jackson*. New York: Van Ress Press, 1940: 195.

21   Cramton, Lewis C. *Early History of Yellowstone Park and Its Relation to National Park Policies*. Washington, DC: Government Printing Office, 1932.

22   Ibid.

23   Langford, Nathaniel P. "Lectures during winter 1870-1871." Gardiner, Montana: Yellowstone National Park, Yellowstone Research Library. Digital Files.

24   Duncan, Dayton, and Ken Burns. *The National Parks: America's Best Idea*. New York: Alfred A. Knopf, 2009: 24.

25   Russell, Osborne. *Journal of a Trapper*. Lincoln, Nebraska: University of Nebraska Press, 1965: 45.

26   Haines, 43.

27   Ibid., 42.

28   Ibid., 46.

29   Ibid., 53.

30   Ibid., 59.

31   Ibid., 106.

32   Doane, 14.

33   Doane, 23.

34   Ibid., 108.

35   Langford, "Lectures given during winter 1870-1871."

36   Ibid.

37   Ibid.

38   Haines, 125-132.

39   Duncan and Burns, 24.

40   Haines, 101.

41   Rugoff, Milton. *America's Gilded Age: Intimate Portraits from an Era of Extravagance and Change, 1850-1890*. New York: Henry Holt and Company, 1989.

42　Lubetkin, M. John. *Jay Cooke's Gamble*. Norman: University of Oklahoma Press, 2006: 49.

43　Ibid., 49.

44　Haines, 86.

Chapter 3:

45　Foster, Mike. *Strange Genius: The Life of Ferdinand Vandeveer Hayden*. Niwot, Colorado: Roberts Rinehart, 1994: 39.

46　Ibid., 12-16.

47　Ibid., 15.

48　Ibid., 28.

49　Ibid., 27.

50　Ibid., 20.

51　Ibid., 22.

52　Ibid., 11.

53　Ibid., 30.

54　Baird, Spencer Fullerton. *Directions for Collecting, Preserving and Transporting Specimens of Natural History*. Washington, DC: Smithsonian Institution, 1852: 12.

55　Foster, 80.

56　Ibid., 117.

57　Ibid., 66.

58　Ibid., 75.

59　Ibid., 60.

60　Haines, 141.

61　Merrill, 27.

62　Kinsey, Joni Louise. *Thomas Moran and the Surveying of the American West*. Washington, DC: Smithsonian Institution Press, 1992: 3.

Chapter 4:

63　Merrill, 39.

64　Ibid., 40.

65　Ibid., 74.

66　White, Richard. *Railroaded: The Transcontinentals and the Making of Modern America*. New York: W. W. Norton, 2011: 24.

67　Merrill, Marlene D. "With Hayden in the Field: A Case Study Based on Unpublished Letters and Diaries from the 1871 Yellowstone Survey," 4.

68 Merrill, Marlene Deahl. *Seeing Yellowstone in 1871: Earliest Descriptions and Images from the Field: With Text by Albert Peale and Illustrations by Thomas Moran, William Henry Jackson and Henry Wood Elliott.* Lincoln: University of Nebraska Press, 2005: 21.

69 Haines, 142.

70 Goetzmann, William H., and William N. Goetzmann. *The West of the Imagination.* New York: W. W. Norton, 1986: 174.

71 Wilkins, Thurman. *Thomas Moran: Artist of the Mountains.* Norman: University of Oklahoma Press, 1998: 83.

72 M. E. "From the Far West." *The Bath Daily Times,* August 7, 1872.

73 Hayden, Ferdinand V. *Fifth Report: Preliminary Report of the United States Geological Survey of Montana and Portions of Adjacent Territories; Being a Fifth Annual Report of Progress.* Washington, DC: Government Printing Office, 1872: 54.

74 Merrill, 128.

Chapter 5:

75 Hayden, 68.

76 Ibid., 128.

77 Ibid., 69.

78 Wilkins, 15-17.

79 Ibid., 95.

80 Ibid., 88.

81 Jackson, 190.

82 Ibid., 179.

83 Ibid., 198.

84 Merrill, 139.

85 Ibid., 177.

86 Hayden, 68.

87 Adams, Jr., Robert (writing as Botanicus). "Exploring the Great West." *The Philadelphia Enquirer,* (September 8, 1871).

88 Merrill, 128.

Chapter 6:

89 Hayden, 77.

90 Merrill, 133.

91 Hayden, 78.

92 Ibid., 79.
93 Merrill, 134.
94 Jackson, 199.
95 Ibid.
96 Waitley, 27.
97 Ibid., 102.
98 Ibid., 23.
99 Ibid., 187.
100 Hayden, 80.
101 Merrill, 136.

Chapter 7:

102 Merrill, 137.
103 Doane, Gustavus. *The Report of Lieutenant Gustavus C. Doane upon the so-called Yellowstone Expedition of 1870.* 41st Congress, Third Session, Executive Document No. 51, February 24, 1871: 11.
104 Hedges, Cornelius. "The Great Falls of the Yellowstone." *Helena Daily Herald,* (October 15, 1870): 100.
105 Ibid., 101.
106 Adams, Jr., Robert (writing as Botanicus). "Exploring the Great West." *The Philadelphia Enquirer,* (September 15, 1871).
107 Merrill, 137.
108 Wilkins, 91.
109 Ibid., 6.
110 Ibid., 91.

Chapter 8:

111 Whittlesey, Lee H. "Visitors to Yellowstone Hot Springs Before 1870." Gardiner, Montana: Files of Yellowstone National Park Heritage Research Center, (1993): 6.
112 Merrill, 124.
113 Merrill, *Seeing Yellowstone in 1871,* 21-35.
114 Haines, *Yellowstone National Park,* 85.
115 Nash, Roderick. *Wilderness and the American Mind.* New Haven: Yale University Press, 1982: 23-24.
116 Ibid., 45.
117 Ibid., 29.

118 Ibid., 50.

119 Ibid., 87.

120 Thoreau, Henry David. *Walden; Or, Life in the Woods.* New York: Dover Publications, 1995: 59.

121 Runte, Alfred. *National Parks: The American Experience.* Lincoln: University of Nebraska Press, 1997.

122 Nash, 69.

123 Gordon S. Wood. "America's First Climate Debate," *American History.* (Feb, 2010), Vol. 44, 58-63.

124 Ibid.

125 Runte, 22.

126 Haines, *Yellowstone National Park*, 85.

127 Ibid., 137.

Chapter 9:

128 Twain, Mark (Edited by Caroline Thomas Harnsberger). *Mark Twain at Your Fingertips: A Book of Quotations.* Mineola, New York: Dover Publications, 2009: 443.

129 Merrill, 264.

130 Guptill, A. B. *The Haynes Guide to Yellowstone.* St. Paul: The Pioneer Press, 1902: 54.

131 Hayden, 89.

132 Ibid.

133 Ibid.

134 Merrill, 139.

135 Ibid., 275.

136 Langford, Nathaniel Pitt. *The Discovery of Yellowstone Park.* Lincoln: University of Nebraska Press, 1972: 24.

137 Hedges, Cornelius. "The Great Falls of the Yellowstone" and "Hell-broth Springs." *Helena Daily Herald*, (October 1870) and (November 1870).

138 Hayden, 90.

139 Merrill, 139.

Chapter 10:

140 Hayden, 96.

141 Ibid., 141.

Chapter 11:

142 Doane, 27.

143 Langford, "Lectures given during winter 1870-1871."

144 Merrill, 265.

145 Hayden, 101.

146 Ibid., 89.

147 Ibid., 107.

148 Ibid., 106.

149 Merrill, 145.

150 Hayden, 110.

151 Ibid., 114.

152 Hamp, Sidford. *Diary of Sidford Hamp*. Annals of Wyoming. Vol. 14: 253-298.

153 Merrill, 147.

154 Hayden, 113.

155 Merrill, 148.

156 Hayden, 121.

157 Ibid., 116.

158 Ibid.

159 Whittlesey, Lee H. *Storytelling in Yellowstone*. Albuquerque: University of New Mexico Press, 2007: 181.

160 Ibid., 180-181.

161 Doane, 29.

162 Merrill, 149.

163 Ibid., 147.

164 Stanley Edwin J. *Rambles in Wonderland*. New York: D. Appleton, 1878: 114-115.

165 Merrill, *Seeing Yellowstone in 1871*, 51.

Chapter 12:

166 Merrill, 160.

167 Ibid., 154.

168 Doane, 31.

169 Doane, 31-32.

170 "Exploring the Great West." *The Philadelphia Enquirer*, (September 15, 1871).

171 Merrill, 162.

172 Jackson, 201.

173 Merrill, 267.

174 Nabakov and Loendorf, 40.

175 Ibid., 108.

176 Ibid., 176.

177 Ibid.

178 Ibid., 154.

179 Ibid., 152.

Chapter 13:

180 Hayden, Ferdinand. "The Wonders of the West-II." *Scribner's Monthly*, Vol 3, Issue 4, (Feb. 1872): 396.

181 "The Yellowstone Expedition." *The New York Times*, September 18, 1871.

182 "The New Wonder Land." *The New York Times*, October 23, 1871.

183 Haines, 155.

184 Duncan and Burns, 12.

185 Nash, 128.

186 Wuerthner, George. *Yosemite: A Visitor's Companion*. Mechanicsburg, Pennsylvania: Stackpole Books, 1994: 27.

187 Nash, 140.

188 Sax, Joseph L. "America's National Parks: Their Principles, Purposes and Prospects." *Natural History*, (October 1976): 59-87.

189 Ibid.

190 Haines, Yellowstone National Park, 110.

Chapter 14:

191 Merrill, 206.

192 Haines, Yellowstone National Park, 116.

193 Ibid., 116-117.

194 Ibid., 118.

195 Ibid., 119.

196 Ibid., 120.

197 Ibid., 121.

198 Hayden, "The Wonders of the West-II," 396.

199 Waitley, 114.

200 Merrill, 208.

201 Ibid.

202 Jackson, 193.

203 Wilkins, 100.

Epilogue:

204 Stegner, Wallace. *Marking the Sparrow's Fall*. New York: Henry Holt, 1998: 131.
205 Chittenden, 72.

SOURCES

Adams, Robert. "The US Geological Survey." *Philadelphia Inquirer*, (June 14, July 25, September 8, September 15, September 26, 1871).

Anderson, Nancy K. *Thomas Moran*. New Haven, CT: Yale University Press, 1997.

Bartlett, Richard. *Great Surveys of the American West*. Norman, OK: University of Oklahoma Press, 1962.

_____. *Nature's Yellowstone*. Tucson: University of Arizona Press, 1974.

Bonney, Orrin H., and Lorraine Bonney. *Battle Drums and Geysers: The Life and Journals of Lt. Gustavus Cheyney Doane*. Chicago: Swallow Press, 1970.

Chittenden, Hiram Martin. *The Yellowstone National Park*. Stanford, CT: Stanford University Press, 1933.

Cramton, Louis C. *Early History of Yellowstone Park and Its Relation to National Park Policies*. Washington, DC: Government Printing Office, 1932.

Delo, David. *The Yellowstone Forever!* Helena, MT: Kingfisher Books, 1998.

Duncan, Dayton, and Ken Burns. *The National Parks: America's Best Idea*. New York: Alfred A. Knopf, 2009.

Foster, Mike. *Strange Genius: The Life of Ferdinand Vandeveer Hayden*. Niwot, CO: Roberts Rinehart, 1994.

Goetzmann, William H., and William N. Goetzmann. *The West of the Imagination*. New York: W. W. Norton, 1986.

Haines, Aubrey. *Yellowstone National Park: Its Explorations and Establishment*. Washington, DC: Government Printing Office, 1974.

_____. *The Yellowstone Story: A History of Our First National Park*. 2 Vols. Yellowstone National Park, WY: Yellowstone Library and Museum Association, 1977.

Hayden, F. V. *Fifth Report: Preliminary Report of the United States Geological Survey of Montana and Portions of Adjacent Territories; Being a Fifth Annual Report of Progress*. Washington, DC: Government Printing Office, 1872.

_____. "The Hot Springs and Geysers of the Yellowstone and Firehole Rivers." *American Journal of Science and Arts*, Nos. 14 and 15 (January to June, 1872).

_____. "The Wonders of the West—II: More about the Yellowstone." *Scribner's Monthly*, (February 1872): 388–96.

Jackson, William Henry. *Time Exposure*. New York: Van Ress Press, 1940.

Langford, Nathaniel. "The Wonders of the Yellowstone." Parts 1 and 2. *Scribner's Monthly*, (May and June 1871).

_____. *The Discovery of Yellowstone Park*. Reprint. Lincoln, NE: University of Nebraska Press, 1972.

Lubetkin, M. John. *Jay Cooke's Gamble: The Northern Pacific Railroad, the Sioux and the Panic of 1873*. Norman, OK: University of Oklahoma Press, 2006.

Merrill, Marlene Deahl. *Yellowstone and the Great West: Journals, Letters, and Images from the 1871 Hayden Expedition*. Lincoln, NE: University of Nebraska Press, 1999.

_____. *Seeing Yellowstone in 1871: Earliest Descriptions and Images from the Field*. Lincoln, NE: University of Nebraska Press, 2005.

Nash, Roderick. *Wilderness and the American Mind*. New Haven, CT: Yale University Press, 1982.

National Park Service. *Exploring the American West, 1803–1879*. Washington, DC: National Park Service, 1982.

New York Times. "The Yellowstone Expedition," (September 18, 1871).

_____. "The New Wonderland," (October 23, 1871).

Rugoff, Milton. *America's Gilded Age: Intimate Portraits from an Era of Extravagance and Change, 1850–1890*. New York: Henry Holt, 1989.

Runte, Alfred. *National Parks: The American Experience*. Lincoln, NE: University of Nebraska Press, 1979.

Russell, Osborne. *Journal of a Trapper*. Reprint, ed. Aubrey L. Haines. Lincoln, NE: University of Nebraska Press, 1955.

Sax, Joseph L. "America's National Parks: Their principles, purposes and prospects." *Natural History*, (October, 1976): 59–87.

Schullery, Paul. *Searching for Yellowstone: Ecology and Wonder in the Last Wilderness*. Boston: Houghton Mifflin, 1997.

Schullery, Paul, and Lee Whittlesey. *Myth and History in the Creation of Yellowstone National Park*. Lincoln, NE: University of Nebraska Press, 2003.

Smith, Robert B., and Lee J. Siegel. *Windows Into the Earth: The Geologic Story of Yellowstone and Grand Teton National Parks*. New York: Oxford University Press, 2000.

Waitely, Douglas. *William Henry Jackson: Framing the Frontier*. Missoula, MT: Mountain Press, 1999.

White, Richard. *Railroaded: The Transcontinentals and the Making of Modern America*. New York: W.W. Norton and Company, 2011.

Whittlesey, Lee H. *Lost in Yellowstone: Truman Everts' "Thirty-Seven Days of Peril."* Salt Lake City: University of Utah Press, 1995.

_____. *Yellowstone's Horse and Buggy Tour Guides: Interpreting the Grand Old Park, 1872–1920*. Washington DC: National Park Service, 2007.

Wilkins, Thurman. *Thomas Moran: Artist of the Mountains*. Norman, OK: University of Oklahoma Press, 1966.

PHOTO CREDITS

PROLOGUE

1JG.Holland.jpg
By uncredited (The Magazine of poetry, Volume 2, Issues 1-4, 1890) [Public domain] via Wikimedia Commons

2mud.volcano.moran.woodcut.jpg
National Park Service: Yellowstone Photo Collection website: "The Mud Volcano," illustration in the article "The Wonders of the Yellowstone"; NP Langford, author; May/June 1871 issue of *Scribner's Monthly*

3Scribners.Monthly.jpg
Wikipedia (Original source: Princeton.edu) (Fair use)

4Bierstadt.Mount.Corcoran.jpg
Albert Bierstadt [Public domain] via Wikimedia Commons

6john.fremont.loc.jpg
Library of Congress website ("No known restrictions on publication")

9nathaniel.langford.jpg
National Park Service. Yellowstone Photo collection website: Nathaniel P. Langford of the 1870 Washburn/Langford/Doane expedition; photographer unknown

10giant.geyser.moran.woodcut.jpg
National Park Service. Yellowstone Photo collection website: "Crater of the Giant Geyser," illustration in the article "The Wonders of the Yellowstone"; NP Langford, author; Thomas Moran, artist; May/June 1871 issue of *Scribner's Monthly*

CHAPTER 1

11yellowstone.river.map.jpg
pbs.org

12CrowIndianOntheLookout.jpg
The Walters Art Museum website; commissioned by William T. Walters

13bison.herd.peaco.jpg
Jim Peaco, National Park Service (from National Park Service, Yellowstone National Park Flickr website)

14bannock.girls.jpg
National Park Service: Yellowstone Photo Collection website

15cutthroat.trout.jay.fleming.jpg
Jay Fleming (from National Park Service, Yellowstone National Park Flickr website)

16obsidian.points.jpg
National Park Service website

17Shoshone.sheepeaters.jpg
National Park Service: Yellowstone Photo Collection website

18wikiup.jpg
National Park Service: Yellowstone Photo Collection website

19sego.lily.renkin.jpg
Diane Renkin (from National Park Service, Yellowstone National Park Flickr website)

20bighorn.sheep.oncliffs.peaco.jpg
Jim Peaco, National Park Service (Yellowstone National Park Flickr website)

22shoshone.indian.alfred.jacob.miller.jpg
The Walters Art Museum website; commissioned by William T. Walters

24california.gold.miners
Library of Congress website: "California gold diggers. A scene from actual life in the mines. Wood engraving in Ballou's Pictorial Drawing-Room Companion, May 3, 1856."

25chinese.miners.jpg
Library of Congress website

26Felled.Trees.Bonner.Montana.jpg
Courtesy Montana Historical Society Research Center: N. A. Forsyth Stereograph Collection (mtmemory.org)

27hydraulic.mining.jpg
Wikimedia Commons: original from Denver Public Library public domain images

28.LAHuffman.with.buffalo.jpg
Courtesy Montana Historical Society Research Center

29nezperce.camp.jpg
William H. Jackson (National Park Service: Yellowstone Photo Collection website)

CHAPTER 2

30lincoln.hall.jpg
Library of Congress website: "Lincoln Hall, interior, from stereo, Washington, D.C."

31nathaniel.langford.portrait.jpg
Photo Courtesy of the Pioneer Museum (Bozeman Daily Chronicle website)

34fur.trapper.jpg
Rocky Mountains Trapper, by Alfred Jacob Miller [Public domain] via Wikimedia Commons

33rockefeller.jpg
Library of Congress website: "Photo copyrighted by American Press Association"

35trappers.currier.ives.loc.jpg
"The trappers camp-fire. A friendly visitor," Currier and Ives, Library of Congress website

36joseph.meek.jpg
Wikipedia (public domain)

37jim.bridger.jpg
Wikimedia; source: Denver Public Library

39henrywashburn.jpg
National Park Service: Yellowstone Photo Collection website

40doane.jpg
National Park Service: Yellowstone Photo Collection website

41cougar.jpg
National Park Service

42a.pastel.canyon.jpg
Thomas Moran, National Park Service: Yellowstone Photo Collection website

43truman.everts.jpg
Scribner's Monthly, November 1871 (procured from pbs.org: "The National Parks: America's Best Idea" series)

44roaring.mountain.peaco.jpg
Jim Peaco, National Park Service

45Cooke.jpg
National Park Service website

47.american.progress.jpg
Library of Congress website

48clear.creek.canyon.train.whj.jpg
William H. Jackson, from Library of Congress website: www.loc.gov/item/det1994008620/PP/

50hayden.andhorse.jpg
William H. Jackson, from National Park Service website

51snowy.mtns.peaco.jpg
Jim Peaco, National Park Service

CHAPTER 3

52hayden.portrait.jpg
Wikipedia (downloaded from USGS Photo Archives)

53joseph.leidy.jpg
Wikimedia Commons

54hayden.insects.sketch.jpg
National Archives

56martha.maxwell.female.naturalist.jpg
Wikimedia Commons

57spencer.baird.jpg
Wikimedia Commons (original source: Smithsonian Institution archives)

58baird's.sparrow.jpg
Wikimedia Commons (uploaded by Dominic Sherony)

58a.naturalist.field.notes.jpg
Museum Victoria (Australia) website
(http://museumvictoria.com.au/collections/items/368920/fieldnotes-charles-mash-maplestone-field-naturalist-victoria-1875-1880)

59dino.teeth.trachodon.jpg
By Joseph Leidy, "Extinct Vertebrata from the Judith River and Great Lignite Formations of Nebraska. Transactions of the American Philosophical Society," via Wikimedia Commons

60hayden.by.tent.jpg
National Park Service

61john.wesley.powell.jpg
By Edmund Clarence Messer (1842–1919) via Wikimedia Commons

62powell.and.tau-gu.paiute.jpg
National Park Service

63armed.texas.rangers.jpg
Wikipedia

64albert.peale.jpg
National Park Service

65charles.willson.peale.jpg
Photo Courtesy of Pennsylvania Academy of the Fine Arts

66sextant.noaa.jpg)
Wikipedia commons (original source NOAA photo library)

68king.darkroom.across.desert.jpg
National Archives: Photographs of the American West website

69whj.by.horse.jpg
William H. Jackson, photographer; National Park Service: Yellowstone's Photo Collection (website)

CHAPTER 4

70ft.ellis.jpg
William H. Jackson, photographer; National Park Service: Yellowstone's Photo Collection (website)

71train.tunnel.whj.jpg
William H. Jackson, photographer; Courtesy Getty Trust Open Content Program, J. Paul Getty Museum (artsy.net)

71a.camp.at.ogden.whj.jpg
William H. Jackson, photographer; Wikimedia Commons (original source: National Archives: record 1116078)

72virginia.city.whj
William H. Jackson, photographer; National Park Service website (nps.gov/museum/exhibits/moran)

75survey.train.jpg
William H. Jackson, photographer; National Park Service: Yellowstone Photo Collection

76portrait.thomas.moran.jpg
Library of Congress: artist Napoleon Sarony (loc.gov/pictures/item/95522072)

77moran.woodcut.grotto.jpg
National Park Service; Yellowstone Photo Collection (nps.gov/features/yell/slidefile/history/articlesillustrations/Images/03144.jpg)

78albert.bierstadt.jpg
Wikipedia Commons

79bierdstadt.lander's.peak.jpg
The Metropolitan Museum of Art online, via Wikimedia Commons

80stagecoach.1869.png
Photographs of the American West: 1861-1912, US National Archives & Records Administration, via Wikimedia Commons

81hunters.expedition.jpg
William H. Jackson, photographer; National Park Service, Yellowstone Photo Collection

82bottlers.ranch.jpg
William H. Jackson, photographer; National Park Service (nps.gov/museum/exhibits/moran/jack8.htm)

83mountains.moran.jpg
Thomas Moran, artist; National Park Service, Yellowstone Photo Collection

CHAPTER 5

85mammoth.today.jpg
National Park Service, Yellowstone NP Flickr website

87canary.spring.peaco.jpg
Jim Peaco, National Park Service

88moran.mammoth.jpg
William H. Jackson, photographer; National Park Service: Yellowstone Photo Collection

91jackson.packing.mule.jpg
National Park Service: Yellowstone Photo Collection (nps.gov/features/yell/slidefile/history/jacksonphotos/Images/14866.jpg)

92mhs.with.two.dead.trees.peaco.jpg
Jim Peaco, National Park Service

93pronghorn.herbert.jpg
Neal Herbert (from National Park Service, Yellowstone National Park Flickr website)

94clarence.king.tif
Wikipedia (original: pubs.usgs.gov/circ/c1050/fig09.jpg)

95devils.kitchen.jpg
"Sketch of descent into Devil's Kitchen; Thomas Henry Thomas, artist; 1888 Daily Graphic"; source: National Park Service: Yellowstone Photo Collection (http://www.nps.gov/features/yell/slidefile/history/articlesillustrations/Page-1.htm)

96survey.bkfst.jpg
William H. Jackson, photographer; National Park Service: Yellowstone Photo Collection

97men.in.tent.jpg
William H. Jackson, photographer; National Park Service: Yellowstone Photo Collection

98palette.spring.peaco.jpg
Jim Peaco, National Park Service

CHAPTER 6

99night.sky.neal.herbert.jpg
Neal Herbert (from National Park Service, Yellowstone National Park Flickr website)

100heliantha.peaco.jpg
Jim Peaco, National Park Service

101indian.paintbrush.herbert.jpg
Neal Herbert (from National Park Service, Yellowstone National Park Flickr website)

104pitching.tents.whj.jpg
William H. Jackson, photographer, photo courtesy U.S. Geological Survey Photographic Library (source: chipeta.wordpress.com/tag/hayden-survey)

102fairy.falls.peaco.jpg
Jim Peaco, National Park Service

105lunch.potato.john.jpg
Courtesy US Geological Survey: USGS Photographic Library (http://libraryphoto.cr.usgs.gov/index.html) via Wikimedia Commons

107wild.strawberry.herbert.jpg
Neal Herbert (from National Park Service, Yellowstone National Park Flickr website)

106griz.in.sage.peaco.jpg
Jim Peaco, National Park Service

109tower.sketch.moran.jpg
National Park Service: Yellowstone Photo Collection

110whj.mixing.chemicals.jpg
Courtesy Scotts Bluff National Monument (source: Scotts Bluff National Monument website)

111jackson.with.mule.jpg
National Park Service: Yellowstone Photo Collection (nps.gov/features/yell/slidefile/history/jacksonphotos/Page.htm)

112stereoscope.pic.whj.jpg
Wikimedia Commons (commons.wikimedia.org/wiki/File:Hot_springs_on_Gardiner%27s_River,_Upper_basins,_by_Jackson,_William_Henry,_1843-1942.png)

113portrait.whj.1862.jpg
Wikimedia Commons (wikipedia.org/wiki/William_Henry_Jackson#/media/File;Jackson_1862,JPG)

114yoking.wild.bull.whj.gif
William H. Jackson, courtesy Scotts Bluff National Monument

jackson.atop.glacier.point
Courtesy Scotts Bluff National Monument, National Park Service

116tower.falls.whj.jpg
National Park Service: Yellowstone Photo Collection

117.tower.peaco.jpg
Jim Peaco, National Park Service

118wildflowers.mt.washburn.renkin.jpg
Diane Renkin (from National Park Service, Yellowstone National Park Flickr website)

CHAPTER 7

120canyon.renkin.jpg
Diane Renkin (from National Park Service, Yellowstone National Park Flickr website)

119henry.elliott.jpg
William H. Jackson, photographer; source: National Park Service, Yellowstone Photo Collection

122brink.of.lower.falls.peaco.jpg
Jim Peaco, National Park Service

123yellowstone.river.peaco.jpg
Jim Peaco, National Park Service

124trumpeter.swans.peaco.jpg
Jim Peaco, National Park Service

125canyon.walls.ekp.jpg
Erin Peabody

126aneroid.barometer2.jpg
Wikimedia Commons

127vintage.visitors.haynes.jpg
Frank J. Haynes; National Park Service: Yellowstone Photo Collection

128canyon.sketch.moran.jpg
Thomas Moran, artist; source: National Park Service, Yellowstone Photo Collection

129canyon.moran.jpg
Thomas Moran, artist; source: National Park Service, Yellowstone Photo Collection

CHAPTER 8

130hot.springs.whj.jpg
National Park Service, Yellowstone Photo Collection

131brochure.alice.wonderland.jpg
NPS/Yellowstone website (nps.gov/yell/blogs/Alices-Adventures-in-the-New-Wonderland-brochure.htm)

131a.wilderness.road.jpg
Wikimedia Commons (George Caleb Bingham artist: *Daniel Boone escorting settlers through the Cumberland Gap*)

132hayden.crouching.jpg
Wikipedia Commons. Original: US Geological Survey (https://en.wikipedia.org/wiki/Hayden_Geological_Survey_of_1871#/media/File:FVHaydenAtWork1870-Jackson.jpg)

133gates.of.yosemite.bierdstadt.jpg
Wikimedia Commons (https://commons.wikimedia.org/wiki/File:HRSOA_AlbertBierstadt-Gates_of_Yosemite.jpg)

134thoreau.loc.jpg
Library of Congress

135walden.thoreau's.hut.jpg
Library of Congress (www.loc.gov/pictures/item/det1994020349/PP/)

136abigail.adams.jpg
Courtesy of the National Portrait Gallery (www.notablebiographies.com/A-An/Adams-Abigail.html)

137jefferson.rembrandt.peale.jpg
Wikimedia Commons

139mammoth.trees.colfax.jpg
Library of Congress (www.loc.gov/pictures/resource/stereo.1s00962/)

140npr.brochure.jpg
Artist unknown; source: National Park Service, Yellowstone Photo Collection (www.nps.gov/features/yell/slidefile/history/brochuresguides/Page.htm)

CHAPTER 9

142bison.wallowing.peaco.jpg
Jim Peaco, National Park Service

143bison.calf.herbert.jpg
Neal Herbert (from National Park Service, Yellowstone National Park Flickr website)

143a.bison.in.snow.peaco.jpg
Jim Peaco, National Park Service

144wolf.jpg
National Park Service

145smoking.scene.peaco.jpg
Jim Peaco, National Park Service

146sulfur.crystals.jpg
Courtesy of the Geochemical Society, Carnegie Institution for Science

147vintage.pool.haynes.jpg
National Park Service: Yellowstone Photo Collection (nps.gov/features/yell/slidefile/history/postcards/fjhaynes/Page.htm)

148swirling.mud.renkin.jpg
Diane Renkin (from National Park Service, Yellowstone National Park Flickr website)

149falling.into.hot.mud.jpg
National Park Service: Yellowstone Photo Collection

150.vapors.ekp.jpg
Erin Peabody

151.sulphur.steam.ekp.jpg
Erin Peabody

152red.spouter.peaco.jpg
Jim Peaco, National Park Service

CHAPTER 10

153pack.train.lake.whj.jpg
William H. Jackson. Source: National Park Service, Yellowstone Photo Collection (nps.gov/features/yell/slidefile/history/moranandotherart/Images/02937.jpg)

155fishing.cone.haynes.jpg
National Park Service: Yellowstone Photo Collection

156camp.by.lake.jpg
National Park Service: Yellowstone Photo Collection

157annie.jpg
William H. Jackson, photographer; source: National Park Service, Yellowstone Photo Collection

159large.lake.view.peaco.jpg
Jim Peaco, National Park Service

160avocets.peaco.jpg
Jim Peaco, National Park Service

161horse.with.odometer.jpg
William H. Jackson; source: National Park Service, Yellowstone Photo Collection

CHAPTER 11

74choppers.poster
Courtesy of Eastern Washington State Historical Society, Spokane, Washington

163lodgepole.jpg
National Park Service

164bluebird.cavity.renkin.jpg
Diane Renkin (from National Park Service, Yellowstone National Park Flickr website)

165wildfire.mike.lewelling.jpg
Mike Lewelling, National Park Service

166porcelain.springs.akin.jpg
Curtis Akin (from National Park Service, Yellowstone National Park Flickr website)

172blue.spring.renkin.jpg
Diane Renkin (from National Park Service, Yellowstone National Park Flickr website)

169mud.pot.peaco.jpg
Jim Peaco, National Park Service

169a.flapjack.camp.scene.png
Illustration from Ernest Ingersoll's book, *Knocking Around the Rockies*. New York: Harpers, 1882

170tree.skeletons.peaco.jpg
Jim Peaco, National Park Service

173hot.pool.closeup.ekp.jpg
Erin Peabody

174hot.goo.ekp.jpg
Erin Peabody

176grand.prismatic.springs.jpg
Curtis Akin (from National Park Service, Yellowstone National Park Flickr website)

178elk.herd.peaco.jpg
Jim Peaco, National Park Service

179.hayden.and.men.tent.jpg
William H. Jackson, photographer; source: National Park Service, Yellowstone Photo Collection

162firehole.river.peaco.jpg
Jim Peaco, National Park Service

181.hotspring.peaco.jpg
Jim Peaco, National Park Service

182men.at.geyser.whj.jpg
William H. Jackson; source: National Park Service, Yellowstone Photo Collection (nps.gov/features/yell/slidefile/history/moranandotherart/Page.htm)

183old.faithful.jpg
National Park Service, Yellowstone National Park Flickr website

183a.closeup.old.faithful.whj
William H. Jackson; source: National Park Service, Yellowstone Photo Collection

184castle.geyser.peaco.jpg
Jim Peaco, National Park Service

185geyser.sunset.jpg
National Park Service, Yellowstone National Park Flickr website

186great.horned.owl.herbert.jpg
Neal Herbert (from National Park Service, Yellowstone National Park Flickr website)

CHAPTER 12

187lonestar.herbert.jpg
Neal Herbert (from National Park Service, Yellowstone National Park Flickr website)

188camp.at.lake.jpg
William H. Jackson; source: National Park Service, Yellowstone Photo Collection

73sitting.bull.jpg
Credit: Wikipedia Commons

189great.springs.firehole.moran.jpg
Thomas Moran; source: National Park Service, Yellowstone Photo Collection

190.grotto.fine.scratches.whj.jpg
William Henry Jackson; source: National Park Service, Yellowstone Photo Collection

191map.geysers.jpg
Library of Congress's Geography & Map Division, via Wikipedia Commons

CHAPTER 13

192railroad.brochure.haynes.jpg
National Park Service, Yellowstone Photo Collection

193butterfly.named.for.hayden.jpg
John Baumann (personal contact)

194niagara.mill.district.jpg
Photochrom print by the Detroit Photographic Co., copyrighted 1900. From the Photochrom Prints Collection at the Library of Congress

196cut.ancient.fir.loc.jpg
Library of Congress

195john.muir.jpg
National Park Service (nps.gov/media/photo/gallery.htm?id=B17BC4E5-155D-4519-3EC6B73FCE2806A8)

197olmsted.jpg
Wikipedia Commons (James Notman, Boston; engraving of image later published in *Century Magazine*)

CHAPTER 14

198oldfaithful.whj.jpg
William H. Jackson; source: National Park Service, Yellowstone Photo Collection

199castle.geyer.moran.jpg
Thomas Moran; source: National Park Service, Yellowstone Photo Collection

200henry.l.dawes.jpg
Wikipedia; original source was the Library of Congress (http://hdl.loc.gov/loc.pnp/cwpbh.04976)

201buffalo.stampede.whj.jpg
William H. Jackson; National Park Service, Scotts Bluff National Monument William Henry Jackson Collection

202slaughtered.buffalo.jpg
Courtesy of the Montana Historical Society Research Center

203bison.renkin.jpg
Diane Renkin (from National Park Service, Yellowstone National Park Flickr website)

204older.whj.jpg
Courtesy of Scotts Bluff National Monument

205grand.canyon.moran.jpg
Thomas Moran; Smithsonian American Art Museum Gallery of Thomas Moran paintings, via Wikipedia Commons

206moran.jpg
William H. Jackson; source: National Park Service, Yellowstone Photo Collection

EPILOGUE

207bald.eagle.peaco.jpg
Jim Peaco, National Park Service

208roosevelt.arch.haynes.jpg
Frank J. Haynes; source: National Park Service, Yellowstone Photo Collection

209for.the.people.peaco.jpg
Jim Peaco, National Park Service

IT'S ALIVE!

01peering.into.dragon's.mouth.jpg
National Park Service (Acquired from NPS-Yellowstone park archivist)

02oldfaithful.jim.peaco.jpg
Credit: Jim Peaco, National Park Service (Acquired from official NPS-Yellowstone Flickr photo-sharing website)

03ashfall.usgs.jpg
U.S. Geological Survey (Acquired from Yellowstone Volcano Observatory website)

04caldera.from.space.usgs.jpg
U.S. Geological Survey (Acquired from Yellowstone Volcano Observatory website)

06fumeroles.jim.peaco.jpg
Jim Peaco, National Park Service (Acquired from official NPS-Yellowstone Flickr photo-sharing website)

07ojo.caliente.spring.peaco.jpg
Jim Peaco, National Park Service

08giant.geyser.jpg
Erin Peabody

09fountain.paint.pot.diane.renkin.jpg
Diane Renkin

10bacteria.like.Taq.jpg
Science Education Research Center at Carleton College (acquired from their website)

11emerald.pool.jim.peaco.jpg
Jim Peaco, National Park Service

12orange.mat.jpg
Erin Peabody

13ephydrid.fly.jpg
National Park Service

14elk.by.geyser.jpg
National Park Service

15riverside.geyser.neal.herbert.jpg
Neal Herbert

INDEX